Sempringham Studies

Russia 1917-1941

Martin McCauley

Sempringham *publishing*, Bedford

Cover picture. A poster by Dmitry Moor appealing for support in 1920 to defend the achievements of the revolution when Wrangel, in the South, and Poland, in the Ukraine, threatened Soviet power.

Sempringham Studies are distributed to booksellers by
Central Books, 99 Wallis Road, London E9 5LN Tel. 0181-986 4854.

Sempringham Books are available to schools, colleges and individuals direct: Sempringham Books, PO Box 248, Bedford MK41 0ZU.

ISBN 0 9515764 5 3

First published 1997

Impression number 10 9 8 7 6 5 4 3 2 1
Year 2001 2000 1999 1998 1997

Designed and set by Sempringham publishing services, Bedford.
Line portraits by Stephen Odom.
Sempringham publishing, PO Box 248, Bedford MK41 0ZU
Printed by Redwood Books, Trowbridge, Wiltshire.

Contents

To student readers and their tutors

Ways to use this book

This book covers a period of great turmoil and change. The core chapters, 4 - 7, outline these changes, give reasons for them and invite you to join the debate on how events happened and develop your own analysis. For comments on how to use information to develop your own analysis and prepare essay answers you will find guidelines in Chapters 4, 6 and 7 of *The Good History Students' Handbook,* Sempringham, 1993, and Chapters 3, 6 and 7 of *Undergraduate History Study - The Guide,* Sempringham, 1997. Do not forget to refer to the glossary, pages 116-19, until you are familiar with the terms used for this period of Russian History.

To understand the History of Russia after 1917 you need to have an appreciation of the condition of Russia before that time. This is outlined in Chapters 1 and 2. Even if you use the core chapters first, you are advised to read the first two chapters before you finish your Russian topic. You may decide to make less detailed notes on these first two chapters.

The second half of Chapter 1 is a full reference chronology, which is a helpful summary of events. A good use of the chronology would be for you to select items and write a working chronology that suits *your* purpose for each of the core chapters when you work on them.

It is easy to read about the past and to forget that it was people, living, scheming, arguing, fighting, who lived through, and made, the events recounted in History books. Chapter 3 focuses on eight main personalities, summarises their part in the events, and seeks to bring them to life.

Chapter 8 summarises the ongoing debate among historians about these years. Information from this chapter is helpful when answers require a historiographical approach.

Chapter 9 provides an overview. In order to gain an early perspective of these years it is a good idea to read quickly this last chapter, for a first time, before you read the core chapters, 4 - 7.

1 Issues and Background

Russia's Past and the Possibilities of its Future

Russia, in 1917, was a backward country in the sense that political, economic and social change had been slower than in other major western European states. Although backward, there had been some developments in the 60 years before 1917. War often accelerates change and Russia had been involved in a massive war since 1914. Would political change be speeded? If so, how would Russia's politics change and how great would it be? Rapid change can lead to instability: if there was quick change, would a period of turmoil follow? With regard to the economy, Russia was late to begin industrialisation but there had been some industrial growth before 1917. Would the pace and form of industrialisation alter, and how would economic and political changes influence society? These are some of the issues which an observer of Russian history would bear in mind. The answers, which are the history of Russia after 1917 (and to this day), are in this book. First, however, what was the condition of Russia in 1917?

Russia

In Russian popular imagination, the country is wide, broad and large. From the sixteenth century onwards Russia was, and still is, the largest country in the world, as far as territory is concerned. During the nineteenth century it was two and a half times the size of the United States and stretched over 5,000 miles (8,600km) from west to east and over 2,000 miles (3,300km) from north to south. Russia was unique in having large parts of its territory in two continents, Europe and Asia. European Russia extended to the Urals mountains and Asian Russia from the Urals to the Pacific Ocean. Most of the population, however, lived in European Russia, and this led to the problem of whether Russia was a European or a Eurasian state. Most of Russia's history has been played out in European Russia, where the original capital, Kiev, and the later capitals of Moscow and St Petersburg are to be found. There was a population explosion in Russia during the nineteenth century and this transformed the country. It grew from about 40 millions in 1815 to about 165 millions in 1913. The government welcomed and regretted this development. On the one hand there were more and more people to inhabit the vast country but, on the other, the Russians had become a minority in their own land by the 1890s. The

Russia, the largest country on Earth

government was shocked to discover that only about 45 per cent of the population regarded themselves as Russian in the 1897 census (millions, according to mother tongue):

The nationalities in Russia in 1897

Great Russians	55.6	Germans	1.8
Ukrainians	22.4	Latvians	1.4
Poles	7.9	Bashkirs	1.3
White Russians	5.8	Lithuanians	1.2
Jews	5.0	Armenians	1.2
Kirgiz	4.0	Moldavians	1.1
Tatar	3.4	Estonians	1.0
Finns	3.1	Mordovians	1.0

The population according to the 1897 census was over 126 millions and the above list of nationalities include only those with over 1 million. There were over 100 nationalities and they included many different races, religions, languages and cultures. The conclusion to be drawn from this was that Russia was an empire and that Russians over the centuries had defeated many native peoples and incorporated them in the empire. This meant that Russia was an imperial, imperialist power and that many nationalities would have preferred, given the opportunity, to be outside the empire and independent. One of the reasons for the expansion of Russia was the desire to improve security. If Russia did not expand into regions which bordered it, other hostile powers might do so. Given the slow communications of the nineteenth century ruling the empire from St Petersburg, perched in the north west corner of the country, was a formidable task. It took weeks to cross Russia, given the few roads. So how was Russia governed?

Tsars in the Nineteenth Century and the Extent of Change

Russian tsars claimed absolute power but they faced one abiding question to which they never found an answer. Can absolute power promote enlightenment and economic development without destroying itself? In other words, is it possible to promote modernisation of the state and society within an autocratic framework? Participation by the population in decision making about state goals is called politics. Alexander I (1801-25) initiated reforms but the goal was to exclude the people from politics. The Decembrists, officers and others from the cream of society, attempted to remove his successor, Nicholas I (1825-55), which led to retreat rather than reform. Defeat in the Crimean War (1854-6) laid bare Russia's weakness, so well conceived reforms were set in train and permitted the birth of politics. However, the murder of Alexander II in 1881 convinced Alexander III (1881-94) that the expansion of politics was dangerous. Violence and terrorism was society's response throughout the century, thus making a dialogue between the rulers and the ruled almost impossible. Russian tsars learned little during the century: at its end they were still claiming to be absolute rulers.

The Revolution of 1905-7

The greatest threat to the Romanov dynasty before 1917 came about almost accidentally on 22 January 1905 when a priest, Father Gapon, led a peaceful march of workers and their families to the Winter Palace to present a petition imploring him to improve their wretched lot. The guards misread the procession as hostile, fired on them and the cavalry charged as well, killing many, if not hundreds. 'Bloody Sunday' irreparably damaged the Tsar's reputation as father of the people. Strikes, demonstrations, spread and the SR terrorist wing became active against the government and in the countryside. Peasants seized land in the countryside. A major factor in the weakness of the state's response was that much of the military was in the Far East, being defeated by the Japanese (the war ended in August 1905). A concerted response was not mounted until soldiers arrived back in European Russia along the Trans-Siberian railway. Had the railway workers prevented their transfer or had the soldiers sided with the population, the monarchy would almost certainly have been swept away. This was the view of Witte. In October 1905 the Tsar issued his manifesto and promised a Duma (parliament), civil rights, including freedom of speech, assembly and worship, the admittance of trade unions, and this was enough for the liberals to change sides and declare themselves content

A cartoonist's response to the October manifesto: the future will be no different than the past with the Tsar continuing to control people's lives

Document: The Fundamental Laws of 23 April 1906

1 The Russian State is one and indivisible …

3. The Russian language is the general language of the state, and its use is compulsory in the army, the navy and state and public institutions …

4. Supreme Autocratic Power belongs to the emperor of all Russia …

7. The sovereign emperor exercises power in conjunction with the State Council and the State Duma.

8. The sovereign emperor possesses the initiative in all legislative matters. The Fundamental Laws may be subject to revision in the State Council and the State Duma only on His initiative.

9. The sovereign emperor ratifies the laws. No law can come into force without his approval …

12. The sovereign emperor takes charge of all external relations of the Russian State. He determines the direction of Russia's foreign policy …

15. The sovereign emperor appoints and dismisses the Chairman of the Council of Ministers and the individual ministers …

78. Russian subjects have the right to organise meetings for purposes which are not contrary to the laws, peacefully, and without weapons …

80. Russian subjects have the right to form societies and associations for purposes that are not in contravention of the laws …

87. If extraordinary circumstances require legislative action whilst the State Duma is in recess, the Council of Ministers may take recommendations direct to the sovereign emperor. Such a measure, however, may not introduce changes to the Fundamental Laws, the statutes of the State Council and State Duma or in the regulations governing elections to the Council and the Duma. Should such a measure not be introduced as a bill into the Duma within two months of the date of its next meeting … it loses force …

98. The State Council and the State Duma are summoned annually by edict of the sovereign emperor …

106. The State Council and State Duma possess equal legislative powers …

---

with the concessions, all of which had been among their demands. They could have insisted on more fundamental reforms but were frightened of plunging the country into anarchy. The hastiness of the liberals was revealed when the Fundamental Laws were promulgated in 1906 and stated that the Tsar was still the autocrat. The Duma was not to restrict the powers of the monarch. One of the most significant events of 1905 was the setting up of soviets or councils. They were spontaneously organised by workers, peasants and soldiers and the most prestigious were in St Petersburg and Moscow. Trotsky became leader of the St Petersburg soviet. The government felt strong enough to use military force against them but Moscow did not give in without a fight. The revolution and the formation of the soviets had taken the Bolsheviks and Mensheviks by surprise and this was symbolised by Lenin's return in December 1905 just in time to see the soviet building burning.

The Russian Orthodox Church

Nicholas I said that Russia meant autocracy, Orthodoxy and (Russian) nationality. The Orthodox Church taught the faithful to obey unquestionly the Tsar who was the head of the Church. Christianity came to Russia in the tenth century from Byzantium but by the fifteenth century the Orthodox Church was free of any foreign influence and regarded Russia as the centre of the true Christian faith. The Russian language evolved out of Old Church Slavonic, used in the Church's beautiful liturgy, and has Old Church Slavonic, Greek and Latin letters. Orthodoxy was not influenced by the renaissance, the enlightenment or any other European intellectual movement. In western Europe there was often tension between the Church and the ruler but not in Russia. By the nineteenth century the Orthodox Church was conservative and impervious to reform ideas but this began to change at the end of the century.

The People

Russia, like other European states, was divided into estates or classes. The 1897 census is very revealing (figures are per cent):

Ruling class (Tsar, court and government)	0.5
Upper class (nobility, higher clergy and military officers)	12.0
Business class (factory owners, merchants, bankers)	1.5
Working class (factory workers and small traders)	4.0
Peasants (rural dwellers and agricultural workers)	82.0

The striking dominance of peasants and small number of workers in Russian society reveal that Russia was only just at the beginning of the industrial era. In Russia industrialisation began during the 1890s. About one-third of rural dwellers were state peasants until the 1830s and then were given land and some freedom but were still taxed. Until 1861 another third of the rural dwellers, called serfs, were the private property of land owners but were then emancipated or freed. They received on average less land than they had farmed for themselves before emancipation and also had to buy the land from the state (which had paid off the landlords). The peasants regarded this as doubly unjust, viewing the land as God's or, in other words, free, and obtaining less land than they had previously farmed. Also remember that population was increasing rapidly so that more mouths had to be fed from the same amount of land. The Emancipation Act was forced on the landowners by the Tsar who feared unrest unless serfs were freed. However, the landlords were successful in revising the original legislation in their favour and this is the major reason why it was so ungenerous. In reality the landlords were storing up trouble for themselves in the future. The land question remained a major political problem. Harvest failures at the turn of the century led to crises and contributed to the Revolution of 1905-7 which saw major changes forced on the Tsar. Redemption payments were ended and Petr Stolypin, the Prime Minister, placed his 'wager on the strong'.

Industry

Russia's industry before the 1890s was mainly for defence, the production of cannon and other articles for war. The Urals, rich in iron ore, was a centre of the metal industry from the eighteenth century. Moscow and St Petersburg had many textile enterprises. However, Russia was a late starter in the race for modernisation. This was a grave disadvantage from the defence point of view because it meant that other European states, such as Britain, France, Germany and Italy, and also the United States and Japan, were capable of producing better weapons than Russia. War, therefore, now posed a threat to the very existence of the Russian state. Coming late was also an advantage as it permitted Russia to import the most advanced technology without having to develop it itself. The huge size of Russia meant that communications had to develop in order to promote industrialisation. Railway building became a major activity and the network expanded from 21,228km in 1881 to 70,156km in 1913. This outstanding achievement was the result of the efforts of Sergei Witte, Minister of Finance from 1893 to 1903 who consciously attempted to catch up with the more advanced industrial states. Since there was little private capital in Russia, the state played the major role in industrialisation, including the attraction of foreign capital. Russia paid a higher rate of interest for imported capital and the state guaranteed interest payments. The Russian state also negotiated large loans from foreign bankers, mainly British, French and Belgian. Witte took the risk of putting the ruble on the gold standard (rubles were directly exchangeable for gold) and it worked because he imposed high taxes in the home market and high duties on imported goods, partly to protect infant Russian industries from foreign competition. Russia consistently exported more goods than it imported and the surplus was 186 million rubles annually between 1901 and 1910. There were 10 pre-1914 rubles to the pound sterling. Recession hit Russia at the turn of the century and this was followed by the Revolution of 1905-7. Industry again took off in 1909 and, between then and 1913, Russia was a boom economy with average annual growth rates higher than those of the US.

Russia's Place in the World

Russia was not alone in the world, it had to compete with its neighbours and, moreover, defend its independence. Napoleon posed a grave threat at the beginning of the nineteenth century but he was defeated at the battle of Moscow, 1812 (Tchaikovsky's stirring *1812 Overture* celebrates this victory). Russia was popularly depicted in English cartoons as a bear. Until the Crimean War (1854-6) it was a friendly, cuddly bear but afterwards it was a hostile bear ready to devour the careless. This revealed that Britain feared Russia as a competitor for influence in Europe and also as a threat to India. Fear of Germany led Britain and France to come together with Russia but this meant that Germany, which bordered Russia, was a hostile power. The agreement was that if Russia, France or Britain were attacked by Germany, the others would come to its aid. But what would happen if Germany went to war without declaring war on any of them? What if one of them declared war on Germany? As it turned out all three declared war on Germany rather than the other way round.

Why was it important for Russia to compete with other European powers? What does competition entail? Before 1914 in Europe it was natural to think of resolving conflicts by military means. True, there had not been a war in Europe since 1870 (except in the Balkans) but the belief was that wars would be short and not very destructive. The industrial revolution in France took off in the second quarter of the nineteenth century and in Germany in the second half of the century. Russia only began in the 1890s. Hence, there was a technology gap by 1914. German industry was much more efficient than Russian industry in supplying the military. Some Russian officers in 1914 were so naïve as to believe they could defeat Germany, mainly because they had more men. Throughout the nineteenth-century reform in Russia was driven by military defeat and the fear that if it did not catch up it might become a colony of the European powers. The major reforms of the 1860s and 1870s which transformed the countryside, local government, justice, education and the military all stemmed from Russia's defeat in 1856. The 1905-7 revolution again accelerated reform and by 1914 Russia was rapidly becoming like other European states. In 1914 Russia had a parliament, political parties, a good legal system, a rapidly expanding banking system, an excellent education system and a growing economy. These were the strengths. What were the weaknesses? The main weakness was the tsarist system itself. Had the Tsar had the foresight to implement a constitutional monarchy as in Britain and to a large extent in Germany, had he been willing to follow the advice of outstanding ministers such as Witte and Stolypin, the monarchy could have been transformed and saved. However, Nicholas II, far from seeing the need for reform, bitterly regretted signing the October manifesto and, thereafter, was concerned to claw back as many of the concessions granted as possible. He even contemplated dissolving the Duma in 1914 - one which was causing the monarch few problems. The weaknesses were highlighted by the outbreak of war in 1914. The army was in the middle of a reform (to be completed in 1917), it was unprepared for war, as was the government and bureaucracy (officials who run the state). Military defeat led to Nicholas's decision to become commander-in-chief of the armed forces and leave St Petersburg (now renamed Petrograd because the former name sounded too German) for Mogilev, headquarters of the General Staff in 1915 was typically ill-judged as he had no military experience and all Russian defeats would be blamed on him. He left the Tsarina, Alexandra, to look after the shop in Petrograd and this was again not a wise move as she, a German, was naturally suspected of not being fully committed to Russia. Ministers who contradicted her were sacked and she was too inclined to take the advice of the monk Rasputin. The kindest thing to say about the government was that it was incompetent and when industrial leaders, in frustration, set up the War Industries Committee, the government would not take its advice.

Was Reform Started from within the Government Possible?

So the conclusion is that Russia had the potential to reform in 1914 but that the monarch, the government and the court did not see any reason to reform. Reform to them meant a loss of power and influence. The Tsar took his oath at his coronation seriously when he had sworn to continue as autocrat. Reform to him meant reneging on that promise. He was not bright enough to perceive that the management of a state experiencing industrial and agricultural development needs to be continually refined. This was partly due to his entourage who had little interest or competence in economics and regarded physical work as vulgar. The monarchy might have blundered along in peacetime but the advent of war in 1914 was a disaster for it. The sheer incompetence with which it conducted the war sealed its own fate. This was all the more frustrating for the pool of talent which was available and was very eager to deploy their skills. The tsarist government and bureaucracy just could not cope with the demands of a modern war. The monarchy is often viewed as tyrannical and this is suggested as the main reason why it failed. It is more perceptive to regard it as so incompetent that it was not able to save itself. By 1914 hardly anyone had a good word to say about the dynasty, it had alienated the thinking classes, the new factory owners, bankers, the lot. It is also true that the level of brain power in the royal family was not very high and that the best brains in Russia had little contact with the court.

Questions to Consider

- What did the Tsar regard as his main duties?
- Why was there increasing opposition to the Tsar and his regime by 1900?
- What concessions did the Tsar make in 1905 and how successful were they in maintaining his power?
- Was revolution inevitable by 1914?

EXAMINATION QUESTIONS

1 Why was Tsarist government able to survive the 1905 revolution?
2 Why did the rulers of Russia resort to repression so often c. 1900-29?

Chronology

Note: Until 1 February 1918 the Russians used the Julian (named after Julius Caesar) calendar. In the twentieth century it was 13 days behind the Gregorian (named after Pope Gregory) calendar used in the rest of Europe. All the dates until 1 February 1918 are given in the Julian calendar. If you want to express all these dates in the Gregorian calendar, just add 13 days. The 25 October becomes the 7 November 1917, and so on. Hence the February Revolution took place in March according to the Gregorian calendar and the October Revolution happened in November, by the same token.

1917

31 January	Strikes and unrest in many parts of Russia, especially Petrograd
10 February	The last report by the Speaker of the Duma to the Tsar in which he recommends a reshuffle of the government and the appointment of ministers who enjoy popular trust
18 February	Strike begins in the Putilov works in Petrograd
19 February	Bread shortages begin in Petrograd
23 February	Demonstration by women marking the socialist women's congress, and is joined by locked out workers of the Putilov works
23-24 February	First worker demonstrations in the centre of Petrograd which lead to armed confrontation with the police and army
25 February	The strike in Petrograd becomes a general strike. The Tsar orders the demonstrations to be dispersed by any means necessary. The troops fire on the demonstrators, causing many casualties
26 February	Duma members refuse to obey the Tsar's edict to disband
26-27 February	The Petrograd garrison mutiny and join the demonstrators. This results in the victory of the February Revolution.
27 February	The Duma elects a 12 member executive committee, with members from all the leading parties, chaired by M.V. Rodzyanko. The Petrograd soviet of workers' deputies convenes for the first time, in the Tauride Palace, Petrograd. It elects a shadow government, a provisional executive committee of the soviet of workers' deputies. It is led by Kerensky and Chkheidze.
28 February	The provisional Duma committee sets up a military commission and a food commission together with the Petrograd soviet. The first number of *Izvestiya* (news in Russian), the organ of the Petrograd soviet appears. Elections to the Moscow soviet of workers' deputies.
1-3 March	Soviets of workers' deputies set up in the leading Russian cities.
1 March	The British and French governments recognise *de facto* (as a fact but not in law, not *de jure*) the provisional Duma committee. The first meeting of the Moscow soviet of workers' deputies. The Petrograd soviet becomes the soviet of workers' and soldiers' deputies after some soldiers join. Order no. 1 of the Petrograd soviet is published and envisages the formation of soldiers' committees in all units to be responsible for the control of weapons.
2 March	The Provisional Duma committee announces the formation of a

	Provisional Government, headed by Prince G.E. Lvov. All ministers are bourgeois (Milyukov as foreign minister, Guchkov as war minister) except Kerensky (SR) as Minister for Justice. Nicholas II abdicates in favour of his son, Alexei, then in favour of his brother Mikhail, who declares he will only accept the crown if offered by the Constituent Assembly.
7-12 March	In his four 'letters from afar' Lenin protests against the article in *Pravda* by Stalin and Kamenev in which they support the defence of Russia against Germany.
8 March	Nicholas II is arrested and with his family is taken to Tsarskoe Tselo (now Pushkin).
10 March	The Petrograd soviet and the Petrograd Society of Entrepreneurs agree on an eight hour day for workers and factory committees are to be set up.
12 March	Stalin, Kamenev and other Bolsheviks, in exile in various parts of Russia, return to Petrograd. They immediately support the policy of the Petrograd soviet and provisional government.
24 March	Bread rationing introduced in Petrograd
25 March	State grain monopoly introduced along with strict price control of food because of the great shortage of food.
29 March-2 April	A Russian conference of soviets decides to support the Provisional Government to the extent that it implements a 'programme of revolutionary democracy'.
3 April	Lenin, his wife Krupskaya, and other Bolsheviks return to Petrograd from Zürich
4 April	Lenin addresses Bolsheviks and members of the soviet on the tasks of the proletariat, known as the April Theses (see page 60).
20-21 April	Demonstrations in Petrograd against Milyukov's note to the Allies in which he confirms Russia will continue in the war and seek to obtain 'those guarantees and sanctions which are indispensable for the prevention of sanguinary conflicts in the future'. The soviet and demonstrators see this as seeking to obtain foreign territory and eventually force Milyukov to resign.
4 May	Trotsky arrives back in Russia from exile.
7-12 May	All-Russian conference of Mensheviks and united organisations of the RSDRP (Bolsheviks) fail to agree.
3-24 June	The 1st Congress of the soviets of the workers' and soldiers' deputies takes place in Petrograd and is dominated by the SRs and Mensheviks, the moderate socialists. The Bolsheviks, the radical or left socialists, only obtain 35 of the 256 places on the executive committee.
10 June	The Ukrainian Central Rada (soviet) declares in its 1st Universal that autonomy for Ukraine is its immediate goal.
18 June-1 July	The Russian army goes on the offensive (the Kerensky offensive) on the south west front, commanded by General Brusilov. By mid-July it has come to a standstill and demonstrations against the Kerensky offensive in Petrograd reveal Bolshevik slogans in the majority for the first time.
2 July	Trotsky's party, the Mezhraiontsy, which was between the Mensheviks and the Bolsheviks, resolves to merge with the

	Bolsheviks and this adds, among others, A.A. Ioffe and A.V. Lunacharsky, to the Bolshevik cause.
3-4 July	An armed demonstration of workers in Petrograd causes the Provisional Government to declare martial law, fearing a coup, and to arrest leading Bolsheviks.
7 July	The Provisional Government occupies the Bolshevik bureau and *Pravda*, Trotsky and Kamenev are arrested and Lenin flees to Finland (11 July).
8 July	Prince Lvov resigns and Alexander Kerensky becomes Prime Minister.
19 July	After the débâcle on the south west front, Brusilov is replaced by General Kornilov as Russian commander-in-chief.
26 July-3 August	The 6th Congress of the RSDRP (Bolsheviks) resolves to drop the slogan 'all power to the soviets' and strengthen the Party as the '*avant garde* in the struggle against counter-revolution'.
1 August	Nicholas II and his family are moved to Tobolsk.
19-21 August	German offensive in the Baltic region, eventually taking Riga (3 September).
25-30 August	Attempt by Kornilov to occupy Petrograd and dissolve the soviet; Kerensky and he discussed this move but Kerensky pulls out and then declares Kornilov a rebel.
1 September	Russia becomes a republic and a five member directory under Kerensky takes over.
8-9 September	Bolsheviks obtain a majority in the presidium of the Petrograd soviet, chaired by Trotsky.
19 September	The Bolsheviks obtain a majority in the executive committee of the Moscow soviet.
25 September	Trotsky is elected head of the Petrograd soviet.
10 October	Bolsheviks achieve an absolute majority in the Petrograd and Moscow soviets. A secret meeting of the Central Committee of the RSDRP (Bolsheviks) resolves to launch an armed uprising. Only Kamenev and Zinoviev oppose this.
12 October	The Petrograd soviet sets up a Military Revolutionary Committee (MRC) to combat counter-revolution. This then permits the Bolsheviks to organise an uprising through the MRC.
24-25 October	The October revolution takes place during the night when troops and sailors occupy important points in Petrograd.
25-26 October	During the night Bolshevik units take the Winter Palace, arrest 13 Provisional Government ministers but Kerensky escapes dressed as a female nurse. The 2nd All-Russian Congress of soviets convenes in Petrograd and confirms the seizure of power as Bolsheviks and left SRs are in the majority. Right SRs and Mensheviks leave the congress in protest. The congress then declares that power has passed to the soviets.
26-27 October	During an all night sitting the congress passes the decree on peace and the decree on land. A provisional Council (Soviet) of People's Commissars (Sovnarkom) is confirmed, headed by Lenin, consisting only of Bolsheviks. It will be provisional until a Constituent Assembly convenes.
3 November	The Bolsheviks finally take the Kremlin and Moscow.

12 November	Elections to the Constituent Assembly begin; SRs and Mensheviks obtain 62% of the votes, the Bolsheviks 25%, the Kadets and other bourgeois parties 13%. However, the Bolsheviks are in the majority in the garrisons and in Moscow and Petrograd.
22 November	In Brest-Litovsk Germans and Russians agree on a 10 day armistice.
26 November-5 December	The 4th Congress of the SRs decides to expel those left SRs who support the Bolsheviks.
2 December	Russia and Germany agree on a further armistice of 28 days. The Supreme Council of the National Economy (VSNKh) is set up to supervise the Russian economy and is subordinate to Sovnarkom.
9 December	The Bolsheviks and left SRs agree to form a coalition government.
9-15 December	The first round of peace talks between Russia and Germany and its allies at Brest-Litovsk.

1918

12 January	The 3rd Russian Congress of Soviets adopts the declaration on the rights of workers and the oppressed people, drafted by Lenin, and contains much which is included in the RSFSR constitution of 10 June 1918. Russia is declared a Soviet republic and a federation of national Soviet republics is to be formed. All power rests with the workers and the previous ruling class may no longer participate in the running of the state.
15-26 January	The Bolsheviks take power in Kiev after a successful uprising against the Ukrainian Central Rada which then moves to Zhitomir.
19 January	The Polish Legion (25,000 men) declares war on the Bolsheviks and occupies Mogilev, headquarters of the Russian Supreme Command (20 January) and Minsk (22 January).
27 January	Germany and its allies conclude a separate peace with the Ukrainian Central Rada.

1 February becomes 14 February as the Gregorian calendar is introduced.

18 February	Beginning of German-Austrian offensive on a broad front after peace talks fail; Russians offer little resistance.
23 February	The Workers' and Peasants' Red Army is founded. Mass mobilisation to save the socialist motherland.
3 March	Brest-Litovsk Peace is signed between Russia and Germany, Austria-Hungary, Bulgaria and Turkey. Russia recognises Poland, Finland, Ukraine and the Baltic region as independent. Russia loses 26% of its population, 27% of its arable land, 26% of its railways, 33% of its textile industry, 73% of its iron industry and 75% of its coal industry.
6-8 March	At the 7th Bolshevik Congress the name of the Party is changed from Russian Social Democratic Labour Party (Bolsheviks) to Russian Communist Party (Bolsheviks) (RCP(B)). The Congress confirms the Brest-Litovsk Peace, proposed by Lenin, by 30 votes to 12, with Trotsky and Bukharin voting against. A commission is set up to draft a new Party programme, chaired by Lenin.
9 March	British troops land in Murmansk and begin the Allied Intervention. Trotsky resigns as People's Commissar for Foreign Affairs and on 8 April takes over the military.

10-11 March	The Soviet government moves from Petrograd to Moscow and on 12 March Moscow is proclaimed the capital of the Soviet state.
15 March	The 4th Congress of Soviets ratifies the Brest-Litovsk Peace and in protest the left SRs leave Sovnarkom.
5 April	Japanese troops land in Vladivostok and begin their intervention in the Russian civil war.
8 April	Trotsky is appointed People's Commissar for War. The Red Flag with the inscription RSFSR becomes the national flag.
13 April	General Denikin takes over command of the Volunteer Army (anti-Bolshevik) after General Kornilov is killed near Ekaterinodar (now Krasnodar).
28 April	*Pravda* and *Izvestiya* publish Lenin's 'the immediate tasks of Soviet power' which demands a new type of soviet official, the reorganisation of the administration (bureaucracy) and the nationalisation of production.
11 June	Committees of the poor (*kombedy*) are set up and to be provided with grain and agricultural implements.
July-February 1919	The Reds (Bolsheviks) defend Tsaritsyn (later Stalingrad, now Volgograd) against the Don Cossacks under Krasnov and the Volunteer Army.
4-10 July	The 5th Congress of Soviets adopts the constitution of the Russian Socialist Federal Soviet Republic (RSFSR). Soviets are simultaneously ruling bodies and social mass organisations of the workers. Workers are given preference over peasants in elections to these soviets. Hostile social elements, the former ruling class, priests, etc. have no vote. There are soviets at all levels, village, city, oblast and at the republican level, the chair of the central executive committee is head of state.
6-7 July	SR uprising against the Bolsheviks in Moscow and other cities leads to the murder of the German ambassador, von Mirbach, and the arrest of Dzerzhinsky, head of the Cheka, but he is soon released. The Bolsheviks suppress the uprising ruthlessly.
16-17 July	Nicholas II and his family are murdered by the Bolsheviks in Ekaterinburg, on orders from Moscow.
4 August	All bourgeois newspapers are banned.
15-16 August	US troops land in Vladivostok and begin their intervention in the Russian Civil War.
13 November	The Soviet government annuls the Treaty of Brest-Litovsk and opens the way for Soviet troops to enter formerly German occupied areas (the Reds fail to reoccupy the Baltic States).
30 November	The Council for Workers' and Peasants' Defence is set up to mobilise all resources for the defence of Soviet power. In April 1920 it is renamed the Council for Labour and Defence (STO) and is dissolved on 28 April 1937.

1919

1 January	The Belorussian Soviet Republic is founded; its capital is Minsk.
2-6 March	The Communist International, the Comintern or III International is founded in Moscow: Zinoviev is elected President.
18-23 March	The 8th Congress of the RCP(B) adopts a new programme, the goal

of which is socialism.

30 March — Mikhail Kalinin is elected chair of the central executive committee of the soviets in place of Yakov Sverdlov who died. Hence, Kalinin becomes Soviet head of state (not a powerful position as power in reality rests with the leadership of the Communist Party).

21 June-7 January 1920 — A great offensive of the Reds on the eastern front destroys the White armies of Admiral Kolchak. The Reds capture Perm (1 July), Ekaterinburg (20 July), Chelyabinsk (24 July), Omsk (14 November) and Krasnoyarsk (7 January 1920). Kolchak retreats to Irkutsk.

11 October — Red offensive against General Denikin stops him at Tula and then rapidly drives him southwards. Voronezh is recaptured on 24 October, Kharkov on 12 December Tsaritsyn on 4 January 1920 and Rostov on Don on 8 January.

4-14 November — Reds bring resistance of Kolchak's armies on eastern front to an end.

8 December — The Allied Supreme Council decides that the Curzon Line is the provisional eastern border of Poland.

1920

7 February — Admiral Kolchak is executed in Irkutsk by the Reds.

29 March-5 April — The 9th Congress of the RCP(B) lays down the economic tasks of the state and adopts the plan for the electrification of Russia (GOELRO).

25 April — Polish offensive (led by Josef Pilsudski) against the Soviet government, together with the anti-Bolshevik Ukrainian government of Petlyura.

26 May-16 June — Red counter-offensive against the Polish forces successful; Zhitomir falls on 7 July and Kiev on 12 June.

19 July-7 August — 2nd Congress of the Comintern in Petrograd and Moscow brings together 217 delegates from 37 countries. The Comintern adopts the 21 points, drafted by Lenin, for admission to it. The headquarters of the executive committee of the Comintern is to be Moscow. The language of the Comintern was German as it expected to move to Berlin after the successful socialist revolution there.

17 November — The Reds take Yalta and within 10 days the Crimea is in Bolshevik hands. The Whites flee abroad, mainly to Yugoslavia and France. The Reds have won the Civil War.

1921

January — Menshevik and SR leaders flee abroad and the Mensheviks set up their centre in Berlin and the SRs in Paris.

22 February — A state planning commission (Gosplan) is established as the supreme planning authority in the country.

2-18 March — The Kronstadt uprising against Bolshevik rule. The island base, in the Gulf of Finland, was of great strategic importance and the Bolsheviks suppressed the uprising of the sailors with huge losses on both sides.

8-16 March — The 10th Congress of the RCP(B) is shocked by the uprising and

	under Lenin's leadership introduces the New Economic Policy (NEP) and bans factionalism (organised opposition) in the Party.
18 March	Treaty of Riga ends war between Poland and Russia.
22 June-12 July	3rd Congress of the Comintern in Moscow with 608 delegates from 52 countries (including 48 communist parties) attending.

1922

6 February	With the Civil War over, the Cheka is replaced by the State Political Administration (GPU).
27 March- 2 April	Despite his declining health Lenin delivers the main speech and reports on the successes of NEP and announces more severe measures against capitalists in the country.
3 April	Stalin is elected General Secretary (Gensek) of the RCP(B).
10 April-19 May	Genoa conference on economic affairs fails to resolve problem of Soviet responsibility form Tsarist debts. It is the first time that a Soviet delegation participates in an international conference. Nearby at Rapallo, Rathenau, the German foreign minister, and Chicherin, the commissar for foreign affairs, sign the Rapallo treaty which establishes diplomatic and trade relations.
30 December	The 1st All-Union Congress of Soviets convenes with 2,215 delegates (1,727 from the RSFSR, 364 from the Ukrainian, 91 from the Transcaucasian and 33 from the Belorussian Soviet Socialist Republics). They adopt a state treaty to establish the Union of Soviet Socialist Republics (USSR). Kalinin chairs the new Soviet executive committee.

1923

4 January	Lenin, very ill, adds a postscript to his Testament, advising that Stalin be removed from positions of power at the centre because of character defects.
20 April	At the 12th Congress of the RCP(B) Trotsky presents a gloomy economic picture and describes the scissors crisis, caused by rising industrial and sinking agricultural prices. (Lenin is absent ill from the Congress, 17-25 April.)

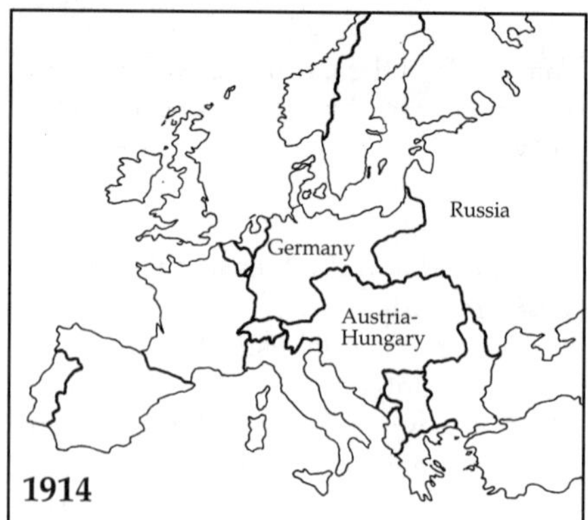

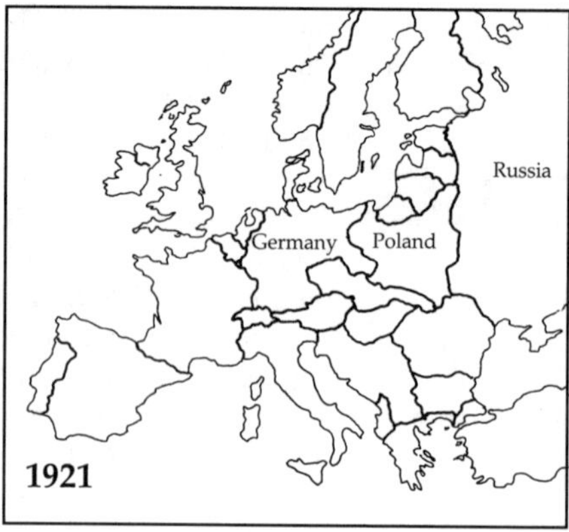

Russia's western border after the Treaties of Brest-Litovsk (1918) and Riga (1921)

15 October	The declaration of the 46, signed by left opposition groups, including E. Preobrazhensky, protests against Stalin and calls for free discussion within the Party. It is distributed to members of the Politburo.
15 December	Stalin opens a campaign against 'Trotskyism' in *Pravda* in response to Trotsky's attacks against bureaucratisation (too much bureaucracy) in the Party and the lack of inner Party democracy.

1924

21 January	Lenin dies in Gorky, near Moscow, and is succeeded by three men, the triumvirate, Stalin, Kamenev and Zinoviev.
26 January-2 February	At the 2nd All-Union Congress of Soviets Stalin swears to uphold Lenin's legacy and presents himself as the leading follower of the dead leader.
27 January	Lenin's embalmed body is placed in a specially built mausoleum in Red Square, Moscow. (It is still there.)
31 January	The plenum of the Central Committee of the RCP(B) resolves, after the great purge of the Party in 1923, to concentrate on the recruitment of workers. On 1 October 1924 it had recruited 241,600 new members.
2 February	Great Britain recognises, diplomatically, the Soviet Union. Many other European states follow.
23-31 May	At the 13th Congress of the RCP(B), Zinoviev and Kamenev attack Trotsky, with Stalin keeping his counsel. Lenin's Letter to the Congress, in which, he comments on the qualities of the leading Bolsheviks, and his postscript, in which, he speaks of Stalin's character defects, are read to the Congress but it is decided not to publish them (they were first published in the Soviet Union under Gorbachev).

1925

14 January	A free labour market is re-established: those wishing to hire labour no longer need to go to official employment bureaux.
20 January	Diplomatic relations established between the USSR and Japan and north Sakhalin is returned to the Soviet Union.
26 January	A Party Central Committee (CC) plenum dismisses Trotsky as chair of the Revolutionary War Council and as People's Commissar for War and appoints Frunze to succeed him.
1 March	A marriage law states that women have the right to retain their surname after marriage but that both partners must agree beforehand on the family name as double-barrelled names are not permitted. They must also agree on the surname of their children.
10 April	Tsaritsyn is renamed Stalingrad
14 April	Bukharin, in an article in *Pravda* encourages the peasants to enrich themselves and states that they need not fear any restrictive measures against them.
27-29 April	At the 15th Conference of the RCP(B) Stalin's concept of socialism in one country is adopted against the opposition of Trotsky, Kamenev and Zinoviev.
13 May	The Turkmen and Uzbek Soviet Republics join the USSR.

10 July	TASS is set up (the telegraphic agency of the Soviet Union) as the official information source of information.
12 October	German-Soviet economic and trade treaty is signed, affording the USSR long term credits.
18-31 December	The 14th Party Congress in Moscow adopts Stalin's views on industrialisation, a new Party statute (renaming the Party, the Communist Party of the Soviet Union (Bolsheviks)), condemns Kamenev and Zinoviev (new opposition) in their protest against Stalin's socialism in one country concept.

1926

1 January	The CPSU(B) has 1,078,185 members (638,355 full members and 439,830 candidate members), of which 750,000 are in the RSFSR, 167,000 in Ukraine and 16,000 are in Belorussia.
4 January	Zinoviev is replaced by Sergei Kirov as Party leader in Leningrad.
10 February	Kamenev, who lost his position as deputy chair of Sovnarkom after the 14th Party Congress and was made commissar for trade, publishes a new economic programme which corresponds to the resolutions of the Congress.
6-9 April	At a CC plenum Trotsky and Kamenev argue for the more rapid growth of industry against the official Party line.
14-23 July	At a joint plenum of the CC and the Central Control Commission (CCC) Trotsky presents the declaration of the 13, opposing the Stalin group in the leadership. The argument for more rapid industrialisation is rejected and Zinoviev is removed from the Politburo.
23 and 26 October	At a joint plenum of the CC and the CCC Trotsky is voted off the Politburo, Zinoviev ceases to be head of the Comintern and Kamenev is removed as a candidate member of the Politburo.
17-31 December	The first Soviet census reveals that the population is 147 million or 13 million more than in 1923: 18% of the population is urban and 82% rural. There are only 31 cities with a population of over 100,000 but the rapid growth of the urban population, it grew annually at 5% over the years 1923-6, reveals the rapid economic changes underway.

1927

1 January	Russian industrial production is now 11% and heavy industry 22% above that of 1913. Privately owned factories only account for 24% of the global output. Agriculture is still below the 1913 level despite the fact that the arable (cultivated) area is now 110.2 million ha, compared to 105 million ha in 1913. However, 28.3% of the 25 million farms have no draught power (horses, oxen) and 31.6% have no agricultural implements or equipment.
12 May	The British police raid the Arcos (All-Russian Co-operative Society) building in London searching for incriminating evidence. There are anti-British demonstrations in Moscow and this results in Britain breaking off diplomatic relations with the Soviet Union (re-established on 3 October 1929).
9 August	After 12 days of debate in a joint plenum of the CC and CCC,

	Trotsky, Kamenev and Zinoviev defend their views and the exclusion of Trotsky and Zinoviev from the CC is overturned but they receive a severe reprimand.
3 September	The leaders of the opposition again send a letter to the CC, signed by 13 of them, criticising the Party leadership and demanding a debate within the Party.
21-23 October	At a joint plenum of the CC and CCC Trotsky and Zinoviev are expelled from the CC because of their continuing opposition to Party policy.
12-14 November	A joint plenum of the CC and CCC expels Trotsky and Zinoviev from the Party and Kamenev and others from the CC and the CCC.
2-19 December	The 15th Party Congress confirms the expulsion of Trotsky and Zinoviev from the Party and Kamenev and another 74 opposition figures lose their Party membership and the same fate is meted out to 23 members of the 'anti-revolutionary' group lead by Sapronov. The Congress decides on the collectivisation of agriculture and the drafting of a five year plan for the Soviet economy. The main victor is Stalin.

1928

10 January	The GPU deports 30 members of opposition groups from Moscow.
16 January	Trotsky is told to leave Moscow and go to Verny (later Alma Ata, now Almaty), Kazakhstan, on the Soviet-Chinese frontier.
27 January	Kamenev and Zinoviev confess their errors in *Pravda,* declare they no longer belong to the opposition.

Agricultural production in 1927 was still less than in 1913

18 May-6 July	Moscow trial of 53 engineers and technicians from the Donbass accused of anti-Soviet activities ends with five death sentences and long periods of imprisonment for others. The trial reveals the growing tension between the state and specialists.

1929

18 January	Stalin succeeds in the Politburo in forcing through the banishment of Trotsky from the Soviet Union, against the opposition of Bukharin, Rykov and Tomsky. Trotsky leaves Alma Ata on 22 January and is to cross the Soviet-Turkish border to Constantinople. On 10 February he leaves Odessa by boat accompanied by his wife and his elder son.
16-23 April	A CC plenum agrees measures against the Right Opposition in the Party and prepares a purge of members.
23-29 April	The 16th Party Congress adopts the first Five Year Plan (FYP) for the development of the economy (eventually the first FYP ran from 1 October 1928 to 31 December 1932) and condemns the right deviation (Bukharin and Rykov) as a great danger to the Party.
25 November	Bukharin, Rykov and Tomsky declare that they will obey the CC.

1930

30 January	A CC decree on the liquidation of kulak farms and the speeding up of collectivisation. Kulaks are not allowed to join kolkhozes (collective farms) as they are regarded as hostile social elements and must leave areas which have been collectivised. All kulak property can be confiscated without compensation.
2 March	In an article in *Pravda,* 'Dizzy with Success', Stalin chastises those who have forced peasants into collectives and permits them to leave if they so desire. They rush out of the kolkhozes but Stalin's move is only tactical as his goal was to ensure that the spring sowing would not be interrupted. Later the peasants are recollectivised.
1 April	The number of unemployed is 1,081,000 or 700,000 less than a year earlier when unemployment reached its peak.
26 June-13 July	The 16th Party Congress confirms rapid collectivisation and measures against right deviationists.
4 November	The homes of Rykov, Bukharin and Tomsky are searched by the GPU.
25 November-7 December	Trial of 'industrial party' members who are accused of promoting armed foreign intervention (especially by France).
19 December	Molotov succeeds Rykov as chair of Sovnarkom.

1931

1-9 March	Moscow Menshevik trial involving former leaders of the right wing of the RSDRP (Sukhanov and Groman), accused of conspiring with *émigré* Mensheviks against the Soviet Union, results in long prison sentences. David Ryazanov, a well known Marxist theoretician and director of the Marx Engels Institute is dismissed and expelled from the Party.
8-17 March	The 6th Congress of Soviets elects Bukharin, Rykov, Tomsky and

Krupskaya (Lenin's widow) and other members of the former opposition to the central executive committee after Stalin declares that the struggle against the Right Opposition has ended.

15 June — A CC plenum decides on the construction of the Moscow underground, the Metro. Work begins in 1932 and the first stretch (11.6km long with 13 stations) is opened on 15 May 1935.

1932

21 January-25 July — The Soviet Union seeks to establish friendly relations with all states along its borders and resolve all existing problems. This policy had already produced results with treaties of friendship and neutrality having been signed with Turkey (17 December 1925), Lithuania (28 September 1926), Iran (1 October 1927) and with Afghanistan (24 June 1931). Further treaties are signed with Finland (21 January 1932), Latvia (5 February), Estonia (4 May) and Poland (25 July). The treaty with France (29 November) gives the Soviet Union indirect access to the Little Entente in east Central Europe and the Balkan Pact in south east Europe.

20 February — *Pravda* published a decree of the central executive committee of the Soviets depriving Trotsky and a group of *émigré* Mensheviks of their Soviet citizenship because of counter-revolutionary activity and prohibits them from ever returning to the Soviet Union.

9 October — Twenty members of the Ryutin group are expelled from the Party for conspiring with kulaks to restore capitalism.

27 December — Internal passport system is introduced in cities so as to clear them of kulaks and speculators. The system is run by the GPU. Those in the countryside were not given internal passports until the 1960s. It was illegal to move to another place of residence in the Soviet Union without a passport.

1933

19 April — British Metropolitan Vickers engineers are sentenced after a trial in which they were accused of industrial sabotage. Britain imposes economic sanctions on the Soviet Union and, as a result, their sentences are quashed. Normal economic relations resume on 1 July.

16-17 November — The USA and the Soviet Union agree on the establishment of diplomatic relations after long negotiations between President Roosevelt and Chicherin, the foreign affairs commissar.

19 December — The Politburo decrees a reorientation of Soviet foreign policy because of the threatening situation in Europe and the Far East. It decides to join the League of Nations and join collective security pacts.

1934

1 January — The second FYP (1933-7) is published which foresees the completion of socialist reconstruction.

12 January — The Party purge reveals that about 300,000 members in Siberia and the Soviet Far East (15.6% of the total membership) have been expelled.

18-23 January	The 12th Congress of the Communist Party of Ukraine resolves to move the capital from Kharkov to Kiev.
26 January-10 February	The 17th Party Congress (the Congress of the Victors) meets in Moscow and Stalin delivers the main speech and states that the Soviet Union has been transformed from an agrarian country into an industrial state.
16 April	The title Hero of the Soviet Union is introduced.
10 July	The reorganisation of the GPU into the People's Commissariat of Internal Affairs (NKVD) begins. The new commissariat is responsible for the domestic police and security abroad.
18 September	The Soviet Union joins the League of Nations and is made a permanent member.
1 December	Sergei Kirov, Party leader in Leningrad, is murdered and Stalin uses this act to begin a period of mass terror.
16 December	Kamenev and Zinoviev are arrested in the wake of Kirov's murder.
29 December	The murderer of Kirov and 13 others are sentenced to death and executed.

1935

15-17 January	Kamenev, Zinoviev and others are accused of treason but Kamenev only gets five years' imprisonment and Zinoviev 10 years. 76 supporters of Zinoviev are exiled to Siberia.
21 March	The NKVD states that 1,074 persons from Leningrad have been exiled for life to Siberia.
23 March	Japan and the USSR sign a treaty in which the Soviets sell their railway in Manchuria (the Chinese Eastern Railway) to the government of Manchukuo (a Japanese puppet state) for 140,000,000 yen.
29 March	British Foreign Secretary Anthony Eden (later Lord Avon) arrives in Moscow to see Stalin, who attempts to convince him and the western powers to enter a collective security system against Hitler.
25 July-20 August	The 7th Comintern Congress meets in Moscow, attended by 510 delegates. The dangerous international situation leads to the adoption of a popular front strategy.
30 and 31 August	Aleksei Stakhanov, a miner, creates a new record by mining 102 tonnes of coal in one shift, equivalent to 13 norms. The Stakhanov movement is used to promote rising labour productivity during socialist construction. (It is admitted under Gorbachev that the record was a sham as many workers helped him and all the machinery functioned.)
22 September	Ranks are introduced in the Red Army (they were abolished on 16 December 1917).

1936

14 January	The exchange of Party books permits another purge of Party members.
18 June	Maksim Gorky, the writer, dies in Moscow and is buried in the Kremlin wall on 20 June.
27 June	Decree banning abortion and promoting the family. The family becomes again the basis of society.

19-24 August	First Moscow show trial (the trial of the 16) against the terrorist Trotsky-Zinoviev centre. The main defendants are Kamenev and Zinoviev and are sentenced to death and executed, Tomsky commits suicide on 23 August.
26 September	G. Yagoda is replaced by N. Ezhov as People's Commissar for Internal Affairs and this begins a purge in the police and security forces.
25 November	Germany and Japan sign the Anti-Comintern Pact in Berlin which includes the agreement not to sign a treaty with the Soviet Union without the permission of the other country.
5 December	A new Soviet constitution is adopted at the 8th Congress of Soviets which abolishes the three class elector system (workers, peasants, intelligentsia) and introduces the general and equal right to vote and direct elections to all soviets. The USSR Supreme Soviet is to consist of two houses, Soviet of the Union and Soviet of Nationalities. The number of Soviet republics increases from seven to 11 with the dissolution of the Transcaucasian Federal Socialist Republic and the appearance of Azerbaijan, Armenia and Georgia as Soviet republics. Kazakhstan and Kirgizia are upgraded from Autonomous Republics to Union republics.

1937

1 January	The ruble which has hitherto been based on the French franc (1 ruble = 3 francs) is now based on the US dollar (1$ = 5 rubles 30 kopeks).
23-30 January	Second Moscow show trial against 17 members of the 'anti-Soviet Trotskyist parallel centre'. 13 are sentenced to death and shot (1 February) and the others to 10 years' imprisonment.
11 June	The arrest of leading military officers (Marshal Tukhachevsky, deputy people's commissar for defence, and six generals) is announced. In a secret trial they are sentenced to death and executed. This begins a mass purge of the military.
Early September	Soviet troops move into the Mongolian People's Republic to protect it against a possible Japanese attack.
16 December	Eight Soviet officials, mainly leaders of national minorities (Jews, Armenians) are accused of spying and treason, sentenced to death and executed.

1938

12-19 January	First session of the newly elected USSR Supreme Soviet. M.I. Kalinin is elected chair of the Presidium of the Supreme Soviet (head of state). The central executive committee of the USSR is then dissolved, having been the supreme state body between Soviet Congresses since 1922.
2-13 March	Third Moscow show trial against the 'anti-Soviet bloc of the right and the Trotskyists' involving 21 defendants, including Rykov and Bukharin. On 13 March 18 are sentenced to death and executed on 15 March.
14 April	The Trans-Siberian railway can no longer be used for international trade and no visas will be issued for travel on it.

29 June — First non-stop flight from Moscow to Vladivostok (7,600km covered in 24.5 hours).

29 July-11 August — A Japanese attack around Lake Khasan, near Vladivostok, is repulsed by the Red Army. (The Japanese attack was in response to the Soviet occupation of a part of Manchuria.)

1 December — After the appointment of Anastas Mikoyan as people's commissar for trade, the Soviet Union plans a rapid expansion of foreign trade with the Baltic States, Finland, Poland and Iran.

8 December — N. Ezhov, notorious for his role in the Moscow show trials, resigns as people's commissar for internal affairs and is succeeded by Lavrentiya Beria.

15 December — A decree on the income of kolkhoz members states that the amount of kolkhoz income to be distributed as wages is the sum left over after all kolkhoz expenses have been met. This leads to a rapid decline in kolkhoz members' incomes.

27 December — The title, Hero of Socialist Labour, is introduced.

29 December — A decree on raising labour discipline withdraws many of the social gains of the previous years (reduction of wages and holidays, including maternity leave, and the removal of benefits from those who change jobs twice). All workers and employees are to be given labour books (a record of their work performance).

1939

15 January — The Party CC adopts various measures to raise labour productivity in agriculture. In the Machine Tractor Stations bonuses are to be introduced to increase incentives. (This reveals the great difficulties encountered by the authorities to motivate those in the countryside.)

17-26 June — Second Soviet census reveals a population of 190,687,000 on 17 June.

10-21 March — The 18th Party Congress (the Party Congress of the completion of the victory of socialism) adopts the guidelines for the third FYP and a new Party statute. Stalin states that the goal is to catch up and surpass the developed capitalist countries and the construction of a classless socialist society.

3 May — Litvinov (a Jew) resigns as people's commissar for foreign affairs and is succeeded by Vyacheslav Molotov.

11 May — Beginning of battle of Khalkin-Gol, on the Soviet-Mongolian border, with Japan, Moscow emerges the winner on 15 September.

11-23 August — British and French military officials negotiate in Moscow and they agree that in case of war the Soviet Union may occupy the Baltic States. No overall agreement is reached as Poland refuses to allow Soviet troops to cross its territory.

23 August — Molotov and von Ribbentrop, German foreign minister, sign in Moscow the German-Soviet non-aggression pact, having already signed a trade and credit agreement (19 August). In a secret protocol the two sides divide up east central Europe. The Soviet Union acquires Finland, the Baltic States (except Lithuania), eastern Poland and Bessarabia. On 28 September 1939 another agreement gave Moscow Lithuania. (The existence of this secret protocol was

denied by Moscow until the late Gorbachev era.)

1 September — Germany attacks Poland and penetrates up to the line agreed in the secret protocol and the Second World War begins.

17 September — Soviet troops begin their march into eastern Poland (as agreed by the secret protocol). Lvov falls to them on 21-22 September.

21-23 September — German troops withdraw to the agreed demarcation line.

28 September — Molotov and von Ribbentrop sign in Moscow a new German-Soviet border and friendship treaty which lays down a new demarcation line on the Bug on the river Vistula. Lithuania becomes part of the Soviet zone of influence.

28 September-10 October — The Soviet Union signs agreements with Estonia (28 September), Latvia (5 October) and Lithuania (10 October) which permit Soviet bases on their territories. A similar agreement with Finland is not reached (11-12 October).

26-28 October — The Soviet occupied west Ukraine, formerly in east Poland, votes to introduce Soviet power and to join the Ukrainian Soviet Socialist Republic. The Belorussian population of former east Poland do the same and become part of the Belorussian Soviet Socialist Republic on 28-30 October.

16 November — German-Soviet agreement on the return to Germany of Germans from the former east Poland, now in the Soviet Union.

27 November — After the failure of Finnish-Soviet negotiations to establish a mutual assistance pact (Finland refused to permit Soviet bases on its territory), Moscow declares the non-aggression of 21 January 1932 null and void and breaks off diplomatic relations on 28 November.

30 November-12 March 1940 — The Soviet-Finnish (or Winter) war begins with an air raid over Helsinki and the march of Soviet troops into Karelia. A Finnish People's Government, composed of Finnish *émigré* communists, headed by Otto Kuusinen, is announced by Molotov. Had Finland fallen, this government would have taken over the country.

14 December — The League of Nations rules that the Soviet Union was the aggressor in the war with Finland and excludes it from the League.

1940

11-12 March — Finland concedes Soviet demands at peace negotiations in Moscow. Finland gives up Vyborg and a part of Karelia. Hangö is rented as a military base to the Soviet Union for 30 years.

10 April — The Soviet Union judges the German occupation of Norway as a defensive measure against Great Britain.

7 May — The Soviet Union introduces the ranks of general and admiral in its armed forces.

12-17 June — Soviet demands to Lithuania (12 June), Estonia and Latvia (16 June) to permit more Soviet bases and to elect governments according to Soviet wishes leads to the transformation of the Baltic States into Soviet republics (21-22 July) and then as part of the Soviet Union (3-6 August).

26 June — The Soviet government demands that Romania secede Bessarabia and northern Bukovina to it. When Romania does not concur,

	Red Army units occupy both regions on 28 June.
21 July	Field Marshal von Brauchitsch, commander in chief of the army, is ordered by Hitler to begin preparing for war against the Soviet Union. Hitler envisages a five month campaign in the spring of 1941.
2 August	The occupied areas of Bessarabia and north Bukovina join the Soviet Union as the Moldavian Soviet Socialist Republic.
21 August	Trotsky dies in Mexico after an attempt on his life (20 August). It is widely assumed the killer was Stalin's agent.
12-13 November	Molotov arrives in Berlin for negotiations concerning the division of the world. Moscow wants Finland, Romania and Bulgaria.
18 December	Hitler signs instruction no. 21, Operation Barbarossa, which envisages all preparations for an attack on the Soviet Union to be finished by 15 May 1941.

1941

3 February	A people's commissariat for state security is separated from the NKVD. Beria remains NKVD head.
13 April	The Japanese ambassador in Berlin, Matsuoka, returning to Tokyo, breaks his journey in Moscow (8 April) and signs a neutrality treaty with the Soviet Union which recognises existing territory and borders and, in the case of war with third parties, the signatories will remain neutral. Japan also recognises the independence of the Mogolian People's Republic.
30 April	Operation Barbarossa is postponed from 15 May to 22 June.
6 May	Stalin becomes chair of Sovnarkom (Prime Minister) with Molotov as his deputy. The latter remains commissar for foreign affairs.
6 June	The German army provides instruction on how to deal with communist commissars (the commissar order). Captured Red Army commissars are to be executed.
22 June	German units attack the Soviet Union across a broad front without a declaration of war. Over 3 million men are involved and behind the army come state security units whose task is to eliminate the Jewish population. Churchill offers Stalin help as does Roosevelt (23 June). Molotov, not Stalin, announces to the Soviet people that Germany has invaded.
22 June-20 July	The Soviet defenders of Brest capitulate after 20 days.
23 June	Hungary breaks off diplomatic relations with the Soviet Union and Slovakia declares war on Moscow and provides Germany with two divisions.
26 June	Finland declares war on the Soviet Union.
27 June	Hungary declares war on the Soviet Union.
30 June	The State Committee for Defence (GKO) is set up and Stalin becomes its head (1 July).
3 July	Stalin, in a radio broadcast, proclaims the Great Patriotic (Fatherland) War and orders that no territory shall be conceded to the enemy.
12 July	Great Britain and the Soviet Union sign an agreement on mutual aid against Germany. Unilateral peace negotiations or armistices are ruled out.

18 July	Stalin, in a telegram, demands the establishment of a second front against Hitler. The Soviet Union and the Czechoslovak government in exile, sign an agreement in London establishing diplomatic relations and mutual aid against Germany, including Czechoslovak units on Soviet territory. Similar agreements are signed with the governments in exile of Yugoslavia (22 July), Poland (30 July), Greece (5 August), Norway (5 August), Belgium (7 August) and France (20 September).
19 July	Stalin assumes control of the people's commissariat for defence and becomes commander-in-chief.
2 August	The US begins providing the Soviet Union with material help and, during the next three months, provides goods worth $145 million.
5 August	The Germans take Smolensk and 300,000 Soviet prisoners.
6 August	Polish prisoners of war in the Soviet Union form units, commanded by General Anders.
8 August	The Red Army loses Uman and 103,000 prisoners.
14 August	Soviet-Polish agreement freeing Polish prisoners taken in 1939 to form the Anders army.
17 August	Narva and Novgorod fall.
21 August	Hitler decides that his main goals are in the south and not Moscow.
28 August	Volga Germans are to be deported to Siberia because they are a security risk and the Volga German Autonomous Republic is dissolved.
8 September-20 January 1944	Nine hundred day siege of Leningrad.
16 September	Hitler orders that for every German killed in the occupied areas, 50-100 communists are to be shot.
26 September	The battle of Kiev ends with 665,000 Red Army prisoners.
29 September-1 October	British, American and Soviet officials in Moscow debate military and economic aid for the Soviet Union. The US commits itself to providing in 1942 aid worth $1,015 million (1.015 billion). The first Lend Lease Agreement is signed on 1 October.
30 September-20 April	Battle for Moscow. The German offensive comes to a stop in December and on 5 December a Soviet counter-offensive forces the Germans back.
3 October	In appealing for warm winter clothes for German troops, Hitler declares that the Soviet Union has already been beaten.
16 October	The Soviet government and diplomatic corps moves from Moscow to Kuibyshev (now Samara) but Stalin stays in Moscow.
6 November	Stalin, on the eve of the 24th anniversary of the October Revolution, puts Soviet losses at 350,000 dead, 378,000 wounded and over a million missing.
7 November	President Roosevelt informs Eduard Stettinius, the head of Lend Lease, that the defence of the Soviet Union is of vital importance for the security of the US. The US, Great Britain and the USSR sign an agreement in Washington providing Moscow with an interest free loan to acquire war equipment worth $1 billion, to be repaid five years after the end of the war.
4 December	Finnish units reoccupy Hangö after Soviet troops withdraw.
9-20 December	Soviet offensive drives German troops back along a wide front.

2 Russia in 1917: Politics, Society and Economy

The Government

Russia was the largest country on Earth, with many non-Russians' nationalities, who would have preferred to have been outside the empire, and there was always the threat of foreign powers trying to occupy a part of the country. Russia had few natural frontiers, apart from the Arctic in the north and the Pacific in the east, so it had to guard very long borders. What type of regime could rule such a state? It was almost inevitable that Russia would have an autocratic ruler, a single ruler, and that the military budget would be the most important concern of government expenditure. By the 1890s Russians were in a minority in their own country, so they could not permit much freedom to other cultures.

The Tsar was the absolute ruler and he was responsible only to God for his actions. The word Tsar comes from the word Caesar as does the word Kaiser, the German emperor. Hence the word expresses the grandeur of the role played by the monarch. The Romanov dynasty ruled Russia from 1613 to 1917.

The Tsar exercised his power through three bodies: the State Council, composed of counsellors or advisers, all appointed by the ruler; the Cabinet of Ministers, or government, with ministers appointed by the Tsar and responsible directly to him; and the Senate, which supervised the way the law was applied and acted as a kind of appeal court. All these bodies were consultative. This meant that the Tsar could consult them but was not obliged to accept their advice. Thus, all authority was vested in the Tsar and it was a criminal offence to oppose him or his legislation. This placed an awful responsibility on the Russian ruler, he was literally responsible for everything in Russia. If the Tsar was intelligent and dynamic, he could cope, mainly by taking good advice. If he were not very bright and had little interest in matters of state, Russia faced problems. Educated Russians wished to discuss problems of the state in the press and in books but this was regarded as a challenge to imperial authority and state censorship was strict. Inevitably groups formed, some of them called secret societies, to debate behind closed doors what could not be discussed in public. Political parties emerged from these groups and were eventually legalised in 1905. Those involved were demanding the right to participate in debate with the Tsar and his ministers on how Russia should develop. Nicholas I (1825-55) did not believe there should be a debate but Alexander II (1855-81) did begin a consultative process but was murdered before it could take root. Alexander III (1855-94) took fright and tried to ignore educated opinion. Nicholas II (1894-1918) was forced into consultations but saw them as evidence of his own weakness.

The Opposition to the Government

The Populists

There was always opposition to the Tsar but before the 1870s no coherent set of ideas challenged the autocratic ruler (the 1825 Decembrist revolt by military officers wanted to replace Nicholas I with another Tsar). The Populists (from the Latin *populus* meaning people) or Narodniks (*narod* in Russian means people) emerged in the 1870s and they believed that the peasants who made up over 80 per cent of the population should rule Russia, not the Tsar. Most Populists were from the middle and upper classes and had enjoyed a university education. They were idealistic and well meaning and 'went to the people', the uneducated peasants, in order to enlighten them about how to improve their lot. The peasants were not amused and often turned the young activists over to the police. This dispiriting experience led some of them to turn to violence, to terrorism, as a solution to Russia's ills. If the Tsar would not listen to them in this world they would dispatch him to the next. The Populists split in 1879 into Narodnaya Volya (People's Will), the terrorists, and Black Repartition, which favoured non-violent political activity. People's Will activists plotted to kill the Tsar and any member of the ruling class they encountered. They achieved their goal in 1881 when they assassinated Alexander II as he was on his way to initiate more reforms. Not surprisingly, the reaction of Alexander III was violent and he set out to crush the opposition. The death of the Tsar set back the process of reforms which he had initiated and ended the prospect of peaceful change. It also resulted in many members of Black Repatriation emigrating to western Europe to avoid ending up in jail. The Populists failed but left a valuable legacy. Many Populists later became Marxists and others were inspired by the protest movement. The concept of an agrarian revolution was very appealing to many, even though it was unrealistic, given the fact that most peasants did not want to overthrow the Tsarist system, but merely to acquire more land.

The Social Revolutionaries (SRs)

The SRs emerged from the Populists during the 1890s when the first phase of industrialisation occurred in Russia. They were inspired by the thought that the new workers (all former peasants) could be attracted to revolutionary activity, indeed they wished to appeal to everyone who thought they would be better off without the Tsar and his system. They can be called agrarian socialists but were not Marxists, who concentrate on urban workers. They believed there should be no private ownership of land but that it should be owned in common. It should be worked by individual peasant families who should have enough land to feed themselves. The Social Revolutionary Party was set up in 1901 and was illegal, as was every political party before 1905. Again it consisted of those who believed terrorism was the most effective form of political activity and those who advocated peaceful protest. Between 1901 and 1905 the terrorist wing dominated and murdered about 2,000 members of the establishment, including Plehve, the Minister of the Interior, and Grand Duke Sergei, the Tsar's uncle. This led to the quip that Russia was an autocracy tempered by assassination.

The programme of the SRs (November 1905) advocated the socialisation of all privately owned land, which would be placed at the disposal of 'democratically organised communes'. This included the confiscation of all monastery, crown and government land. The party called for the summoning of a Constituent Assembly to abolish autocracy and to replace it with a modern system. The goal was a democratic republic with wide autonomy for regions, rural and urban settlements, the right of national self-determination for minorities and the democratic election of all officials.

The Social Democrats (SDs)

All social democrats before 1917 were Marxists and social democratic parties were established in most European states. The exception was Britain where the party of the working class became known as the Labour Party, a non-Marxist party. Karl Marx (1818-83) was a German of Jewish origin who believed he had discovered the scientific laws which governed human society. He was active at a time when sciences such as biology, chemistry, physics and so on were evolving rapidly on the basis of laws which could be tested by any competent scientist. It was not difficult to believe that human society was regulated by similar laws which, once discovered, would make it possible to solve all the problems of human existence. Marx believed he had discovered the motive force of existence, the class struggle. Society passed through various stages, from hunter gatherers to slavery, to feudalism, to capitalism and then to socialism-communism. Inequality entered the world with private ownership. Thereafter the class struggle was between the haves and the have nots, with the haves becoming a smaller and smaller minority and the have nots a larger and larger proportion of society. Under capitalism, the haves are the land owners and factory owners and the have nots the workers. The capitalists are the bourgeoisie and the workers are the proletariat (Orwell calls them the proles in his famous satirical novel, *1984*). Capitalism would give way to socialism, under which there would be common ownership of land, factories, etc and rewards for labour would be according to productivity.

The higher stage of socialism, communism, would arrive when production reached the position of providing everything a person needed, irrespective of the contribution he or she made to society. The wonderful thing about this model was that it was inevitable, it was scientific. The haves were referred to as the oppressors and the have nots, the oppressed. There was also a moral content to this theory. The oppressors would be punished by being dispossessed and the oppressed would inherit the Earth. Justice would finally prevail throughout the Earth. As you can see there are striking parallels between this theory and religion, and Christianity. This has led some to call Marxism a secular or earthbound religion.

Karl Marx

Marx (1818-83) based his theory on the industrial revolutions in France and England and hence had little relevance to Russia before the 1890s. Then there was an explosion of interest in Marxism and it became chic to say one was a Marxist. The father of Russian Marxism was Georgy Plekhanov, a former member of the SRs, but on the non-violent wing. He was one of the founders of the first Marxist group in Russia in 1883, the Emancipation of Labour Group. Plekhanov lived in western Europe and modelled his elegant prose on the writings of the German social democrats. He adopted their view of an evolutionary path to revolution but Plekhanov also introduced the idea of an élite from the upper class adopting Marxism and bringing it to the proletariat. In other words, the working class would not be led by workers but by members of the intelligentsia, the educated class. The Russian Social Democratic Labour (Workers') Party was founded in Minsk in 1898 but almost all its members were immediately arrested as the Tsarist secret police, the Okhrana, had penetrated the movement. Its IInd Congress, in Brussels and then London, after the Belgian authorities had sent the Russians packing, was the real founding congress and resulted in the famous split which gave birth to the Bolsheviks and Mensheviks. There was a confrontation at the congress between Plekhanov (who did his level best to avoid conflict) and Vladimir Ilich Ulyanov, better known as Lenin. Lenin was quite determined to bring Plekhanov's leadership into question. Plekhanov preferred reform to revolution and Lenin the reverse. Lenin chose to challenge Plekhanov on who could be a member of the party. Plekhanov supported the usual west European view of a broadly based party, where a member could be anyone who accepted the party programme and paid his or her dues. Lenin preferred a tightly knit group of professional revolutionaries who lived, drank, slept and dreamed revolution. Sex was way down the list of priorities. The sharpest exchanges were between Lenin and Yuly Martov, defending the Plekhanov line. The congress was almost evenly divided between the two camps but after a few votes had gone in his favour, Lenin, ever the great opportunist, argued that his supporters were in the majority, in Russian, the *bolshinstvo.* A member of the *bolshinstvo* was a Bolshevik. Martov's comrades were in the minority, the menshinstvo and a member of this group was a Menshevik. The Mensheviks followed the west European tradition of not having high profile party leaders, Martov was recognised by most as the Menshevik leader, but the Bolsheviks, or rather Lenin, took a different line and fought for supremacy and was recognised as leader but not the undisputed leader. The Mensheviks and Bolsheviks parted company in 1912 and two separate parties evolved. Frustratingly for the outsider, they both laid claim to be the Russian Social Democratic Labour Party and most members in Russia until 1917 would have preferred the two factions to settle their differences.

The programme of the SDs (1903) called, among others, for the immediate overthrow of the tsarist autocracy and its replacement by a democratic republic whose constitution should guarantee the sovereignty of the people, equality of all before the law, national self-determination of all minorities, the replacement of the standing (professional) army by people's militias, the separation of church and state, free and compulsory education for all. It is striking that this programme did not call for the nationalisation of all private property.

The Bolsheviks (after the 1905 revolution had broken out) advocated a victorious popular uprising which would establish a democratic republic and a provisional revolutionary government. Bolsheviks would then insist that this government implemented Bolshevik demands for policies which favoured the working class, and also push towards a socialist revolution.

The Mensheviks, in 1905, did not wish to participate in a provisional revolutionary government, which they thought would be bourgeois, and preferred to remain the 'party of extreme revolutionary opposition' until the proletarian revolution succeeded in the industrially developed European states. After the overthrow of Tsarism they expected the liberal bourgeoisie to take over and become the main agent of change. The bourgeoisie had the right to rule until capitalism was well developed in Russia or revolution broke out in Europe. The Bolsheviks, however, saw the poorer peasants as the natural allies of the workers after the overthrow of the Tsar. The Mensheviks thought that the land question should be postponed until the convocation of the Constituent Assembly, not a policy likely to win them much peasant support.

The Liberals

Liberalism is non-revolutionary and advocates evolutionary reforms, based on the rights of the individual, private property, the rule of law, democracy (the right of all to participate in the debate about the running of the state, normally through a parliament) and pluralism (there is no single model for the development of society). The above reveals the limited impact of liberalism in Russia as the country was only just undergoing industrialisation. Fundamental to the growth of liberalism is the market economy which permits individuals and groups to become entrepreneurs or business people. For a market economy to develop, political and social stability are necessary, and the legal system needs to function well as this is the guarantee that contracts will be honoured. The market economy provides a demand for the professions, lawyers, accountants, doctors, dentists, and the new consumers are able to pay for their services. These professionals often vote liberal. They belong to the growing middle class. Some national minorities found the liberals attractive as a vehicle for articulating their desire to leave the empire.

The liberals were concentrated in the Constitutional Democrat Party (Kadets from the initials KD, constitutional democrats in Russian). The Kadets modelled themselves on the British Liberal Party and advocated a constitutional monarchy (one bound by a constitution), which would share power with a democratically elected constituent assembly (a parliament elected by everyone). A Duma or parliament did come into being in 1905 but it is significant that when the monarch was overthrown in 1917 the cry went up for a Constituent Assembly and it was eventually elected in late 1917. Liberals also called for equality and civil rights for all citizens (Jews before 1905, for instance, were not permitted to stay overnight in St Petersburg), the abolition of censorship, the ending of redemption payments by the peasants, the right to organise in trade unions and other associations, the right to strike, and the introduction of free, universal education. The liberal leaders were often from the professions and the universities. Paul Milyukov, their most influential leader, was a professor of history.

The programme of the Kadets (1905) laid down fundamental civil rights, equality before the law and cultural self-determination (the right of minorities to decide in which language to communicate and develop their culture), the election of a parliament, local self-government shall be introduced with local parliaments, the death penalty shall be abolished, redemption payments shall be abolished, land shall be transferred from the state to those who work on the land, workers shall be free to set up trade unions and to strike, and there shall be universal, free and compulsory primary education.

Supporters of the Government

The Conservatives

Moderate conservatives were to be found mainly in the Octobrist party, so named as it took its name from the date of the October manifesto, issued by the Tsar, in 1905. Hence, it supported the monarchy and wanted the preservation of the Russian Empire. The establishment of the Duma and the reforms which flowed from the October manifesto were sufficient for the moment. Together with the liberals they feared anarchy (they spoke of the dark masses, the unwashed peasants and workers) and were aware of the fragile nature of the Russian state. Hence, they did not favour full democracy as this would have brought to power those who wanted to end the present system.

The programme of the Octobrists (November 1905) regarded the main task as the establishment of a constitutional monarchy. It called for unity among those who oppose revolution and favour the peaceful renewal of Russia. The Octobrists proposed the unity and indivisibility of the Russian state (no minority will be permitted to secede or leave the empire); peasants should have the rights of all other citizens and peasant land-holding should be extended and regulated; workers should have the right to form trade unions and to strike.

There were two main right wing conservative parties: the **Nationalist Party**, which advocated the unity of the empire, loyalty to autocracy, expansion of the Orthodox Church, especially in the villages, development of local government in Russia to protect Russians in areas where they are a minority, opposition to equal rights for Jews and the development of Russian national self-consciousness in schools. The **Union of the Russian People**. The Union recognised the Orthodox faith as the foundation of Russian life, that the autocratic sovereign was the supreme truth, law and strength, the Russians were the sovereign nation and other nationalities, except the Jews, had equal civil rights, the Russian empire was indivisible, and Jews should be declared foreigners and encouraged to emigrate.

Society and Economy: a Period of Rapid Change

Consider these statistics.

Table 2.1: Changes in significant indices, 1905-13

	1905	*1910*	*1913*
Population (millions)	132.9	160.7	175.1(1914)
Pig iron production (m. poods)	179.1	185.8	283.0
Coal production (m. poods)	986.3	1,526.3	2,200.1
Railways (thous. km end year)	53.2	66.6	70.2
Consumption of cotton (m. poods)	16.0	22.1	25.7
Imports (m. rubles)	626.3	1,084.4	1,084.4
Exports (m. rubles)	716.2	1,449.0	1,520.0
Budget revenue (m. rubles)	1,704.1	2,780.9	3,417.3
Budget expenditure (m. rubles)	1,599.1	2,473.1	3,094.2

1 pood = 36.1lb or 16.38kg

The rapid growth in population meant that some classes or groups in society grew faster than others. If we refer to the 1897 census as a rough guide the ruling class (the Tsar, court and government) only made up 0.5 per cent of the population and it was probably a smaller proportion by 1917, say a total of 800,000 (see page 38). The upper class (nobility, higher class and military officers) in 1914 was less than the 12 per cent in 1897 (because most of the population increase took place in the countryside) but the war resulted in a rapid increase in the number of military officers. However, the composition of the officer class changed during the war because of the high casualty rates of officers, many of them from the nobility. They were replaced by young men from the middle classes, many of whom had no desire to be officers since it meant a short life span. Perhaps this class numbered about 16 million in 1917 or 9 per cent of the population. The ruling and upper classes were demoralised by 1917. The two groups which expanded fastest before 1917 were the business and professional classes and the workers. The rapid growth of the economy in the years before 1914 increased the wealth of the businessmen and this, in turn, made it possible for the professional middle class to increase rapidly in numbers. The industrialists were very frustrated by the incompetence of the Tsarist government in fighting the war and attempted to increase its influence over policy but with very limited success. The war accelerated the conflict between the ruling class, with its wealth derived mainly from land, and the thrusting middle classes whose wealth was from factories, production and trade. In the more developed European countries the middle classes, the new rich, were gradually taking over from the old rich. The business and professional middle class may have numbered about 2 per cent of the population or 3.5 million in 1917. The following statistics demonstrate the rapid growth of the professional middle class by 1914:

- Agronomists (agricultural advisers on crops): over the years 1909-13 their numbers jumped from 2,541 to 9,112. However, the number with an educational qualification dropped from 54 per cent to 43.4 per cent of the total and this reveals the great shortage of these specialists.
- Veterinary medicine: in 1912 there were 3,400 vets and 3,800 assistants (feldshers). In 1914 a different source records 5,200 qualified vets. In 1914 the Ministry of Agriculture reported 5,000 vacancies for vets (this excluded the army and the zemstva (local government).
- Doctors: the 1897 census reported about 17,000 doctors. In 1912 there were 22,772 doctors and 28,500 assistants; 8,100 hospitals with 220,000 beds. In 1914 the Russian Medical Register recorded 42,700 names, including 28,240 doctors, 3,120 female doctors, 5,330 pharmacists and 5,800 dentists. In 1913 there were less than two doctors per 10,000 of the population.
- Teachers: in 1906 the number of teachers with higher education, teaching in secondary schools, came to 11,647; in 1914 it was 20,956. In 1914 along with these there were also 3,185 in private and 3,085 in private schools - a total of 27,226. There were 10 teacher training schools in 1900 and 48 in 1916. The number of primary school teachers in 1906 was 69,200 in rural areas and 2,800 in towns. In 1914 the

numbers were 128,000 and 3,500. The 1911 census of primary schools reported 100,700 schools with 153,300 with 52 per cent of teachers having a secondary school education and 32 per cent of the rest had a teaching qualification. Implementation of the goal of universal primary school education: it was estimated that 370,464 teachers were needed and 307 colleges would be needed to train this number.

The Economy

The rapid expansion of the Russian economy and the demands of the war economy saw a rise in the number of workers from about 5.5 million in 1897 to 19.97 million in 1917. Hence, the proportion of workers rose from 4 per cent in 1897 to 12 per cent in 1917. The following table provides a breakdown of wage earners in 1917.

Table 2.2: Wage earners in 1917

	Type of Work	*Total*	*%*
i)	Workers in manufacturing, metallurgy and mining, of which	3,643,300	18.4
	Mining and metallurgical	810,000	-
	Workers in state owned factories and artillery establishments	385,700	-
	Workers in naval establishments	57,700	-
	Workers in army repair shops and in other enterprises at the front	134,800	-
ii)	Workers employed at home and in urban and rural workshops (*comment on No.)	3,500,000	17.6
iii)	Unskilled and casual labourers	1,500,000	7.5
iv)	Building workers	1,500,000	7.5
v)	Railway workers and employees, of which	1,265,700	6.3
	On lines in use	1,001,500	
	On lines under construction	202,300	
	Railway workshop workers	61,900	
vi)	Water transport workers and employees	500,000	2.5
vii)	Postal and telegraph workers	91,000	0.5
viii)	Agricultural workers	5,000,000	24.9
ix)	Workers and employees in commercial establishments and in catering	865,000	4.2
x)	Domestic servants, cleaners, etc	2,100,000	10.6
	Total	19,965,000	100.0

* This is almost certainly an underestimate; other sources give between 5 and 10 million.

Many of these workers returned to their village to help with bringing in the harvest.

Russia was different from other industrial states in that it had many large factories and few medium-sized enterprises. One of the reasons for this was that factories often had to make almost everything they needed to produce something, whereas in western Europe and the United States many of these parts would have been bought from other factories. This is typical of a country at the beginning of industrialisation. The following table provides a breakdown of the number of factories and workers in Russia on 1 January 1917.

Table 2.3: Factories and workers, 1 January 1917

Region	*Enterprises*	*Workers*	*% of total*
Moscow	4,055	1,000,114	47.6
Petrograd	1,617	345,438	16.4
Kiev	2,329	269,998	12.9
Kharkov-Ekaterinoslav	1,224	188,421	9.0
Volga	1,177	114,250	5.4
Caspian	711	63,776	3.1
Rostov	520	51,241	2.5
Urals	438	45,063	2.2
Transcaucasia	361	15,691	0.9
Total	12,432	2,093,881*	100.0
Siberia	not available		
Turkestan	not available		

*Mathematical error in original

This table reveals the dominance of the Moscow region in the Russian economy with Petrograd only having about one-third of Moscow's workers. The rest of the table demonstrates the spread of industry throughout the country, accelerated by the spurt of 1909-13.

By May 1917 enterprises were predominantly producing for defence and over 80 per cent of workers in Moscow and Petrograd were in defence plants. The labour force of the metallurgical industry grew fastest during the war. This activity resulted in the populations of St Petersburg and Moscow growing during the war.

- The population of St Petersburg in January 1897 was 1,264,700
- The population of St Petersburg in December 1914 was 2,217,500
- The population of Petrograd in December 1917 was 2,300,000
- The population of Moscow in January 1897 was 1,038,600
- The population of Moscow in January 1914 was 1,762,700
- The population of Moscow in September 1917 was 1,854,400

A Time of Change in Russian Society

The number of peasants increased the most rapidly before 1917 but some of them became workers so that peasants.

Hence, an estimate of the social composition of Russian society in

1917, compared to 1897, would be (per cent):

Table 2.4: The social composition of Russian society, 1897 and 1917

	1897	*1917*
Ruling class	0.5	0.4
Upper class	12.0	9.0
Business class	1.5	2.0
Workers	4.0	12.0
Peasants	82.0	76.6

The change in the composition of society demonstrates the impact of economic growth, much of the newly created wealth coming from industry. Hence, as the economy grew so the proportion of workers in society would grow. A significant fact about this development was that workers were concentrated in large numbers in factories, with low living standards, because labour productivity (the amount a worker produces) was also low. A major reason for this was that many operations were performed by hand, whereas elsewhere in Europe they would have been performed by machine. One may say that this revealed how backward Russian industry was but it is sensible to employ labour if it is cheaper than installing machinery. An example of this was Belgian investment in Russia where the Belgians preferred to employ many more workers in Russia than in their comparable factories in Belgium where more machinery was installed to replace labour.

The Stolypin land reform of November 1906 permitted households (there were an estimated 10-12 million households) to leave the commune, put all the strips of land they farmed in the commune together and set up as independent farmers. Stolypin saw this as a 'wager on the strong', those who would have the dynamism to leave and begin farming on their own account. In 1915 about 2 million households had left the commune but some came back during the war.

Peasants gradually acquired a greater proportion of privately owned land in Russia. Whereas in 1887 they owned 12.6 per cent of private land, this rose to 24.8 per cent in 1905 and 30.4 per cent in 1913. The rest of the land was owned by the Tsar, his family, the Church, nobility and landlords. In 1905 13,851 landed estates occupied 60.3 per cent of land whereas 695,248 estates (or 92.5 per cent of the total) only accounted for 16.7 per cent of land. Hence, the vast majority of nobility and landlords owned estates of less than 200 hectares. Before 1914 peasants were buying land mainly from the large estates. Peasants were also leasing land from the large estates and by 1914 were farming a considerable amount of the land of large estates. Another reason for this was that landlords were isolated in the countryside and if they did not lease land could face violence from the local population. Had there been no October Revolution in 1917 it is likely that peasants would have owned about half the land and farmed much of the rest by the 1930s. Put in this light the October Revolution was a disaster for the Russian peasantry.

The Orthodox Church dominated Russian life, in the cities and in the countryside, and it appeared that Russia and religion went together like a horse and carriage. However, the Bolsheviks attacked religion and revealed that it was possible to break the hold of the Church on society.

Russian Culture

The rapid expansion of education after 1900 reinforced the dominance of Russian as the language of culture. French and German were spoken at court but Russian was widely spoken by 1914. A mark of culture among Russians was to speak at least one foreign language. The great flowering of Russian literature began in the first half of the nineteenth century and carried through to 1914 with writers such as Tolstoy, Turgenev and Dostoyevsky gaining a world reputation. Russian art was also *avant garde* with painters such as Chagall, El Lissitzky and Kandinsky. In ballet Diagiliev was known everywhere. Hence, Russian culture was vibrant by 1914 and influencing the rest of Europe and the world.

Questions to Consider

- Political opposition was building up from 1900. Examine the various programmes to rule Russia more successfully and justly. Divide them into those parties which wished to retain the monarchy and those which did not. Why did the socialists want a republic?
- Did the rise in Russia's population make it more difficult to govern?
- Why were the middle classes so unsuccessful in their attempts to influence the Tsarist government between 1914 and 1917?

EXAMINATION QUESTIONS

1 How valid is the view that 'Tsarist government was stable between 1906-14: the Bolsheviks gained and consolidated their power in the period 1917-1922 only because of the effects of the First World War'?

2 'Underdeveloped in every sense.' How valid is this view of the Russian economy in 1917?

3 To what extent was the Russian working class revolutionary in 1914?

4 'The governments of Russia in the period c. 1900-29 suggest that authoritarian dictatorship was the only sustainable form of government.' Comment on this view.

3 Key Personalities: Nicholas II to Stalin

Romanov, Nikolai Aleksandrovich (Nicholas II, Tsar of all Russia) (1868-1918)

A mild-mannered, self-effacing, politically unimaginative, family-loving man, completely out of his depth as Tsar, especially at such a critical juncture in his nation's history. His father, Alexander III, died early of liver disease in November 1894, catapulting the young Tsarevich (Tsar's son) into responsibility for the Russian nation at a much younger age than expected. His mother was a daughter of the King of Denmark. A few weeks after ascending the throne, Nicholas married Princess Alix (Aleksandra) of Hesse Darmstadt, whose mother, Alice, was a daughter of Queen Victoria. After four daughters, the greatly desired son, Aleksei, was born in 1904. However, joy mingled with tragedy, he was a haemophiliac, inherited through the female line. Nicholas II's training, between 1885 and 1890, under the supervision of Konstantin Pobedonostsev, a conservative, ill-prepared him to cope with the rapid economic and social changes under way. He started off on the wrong foot by denouncing as 'senseless dreams' proposals to involve public bodies, such as the zemstva, in government. He shared the anti-Semitism which was prevalent at the court and did nothing to put a brake on the pogroms against Jews. He was forced into concessions during the 1905 Revolution and he always resented Witte's role in this, even though his autocratic powers were confirmed in the Fundamental Laws, April 1906. After the tercentenary celebrations of the Romanov dynasty, 1913, he even considered dissolving the Duma, although it only enjoyed weak legislative powers. After the initial defeats of the Russian Army, he determined in August 1915, to move to Mogilev the headquarters of the General Staff, to become commander-in-chief. His advisers told him this was ill-judged, since he lacked military experience and he would become personally associated with defeat. One reason why he insisted on going may have been the desire to escape from the Tsarina.

He was deaf to all pleas for a government of national confidence and it was only when he was abdicating, March 1917, that he conceded on this issue. His refusal to draw into his confidence those parties which accepted a constitutional monarchy as their goal, the Octobrists and Kadets, fatally weakened them during 1917. When he abdicated he noted in his diary that he read Caesar's *Gallic Wars.* (The Russian word Tsar is derived from Caesar.) He abdicated in favour of his son, Aleksei, but when informed that this would mean parting with him, he abdicated a second time in favour of his brother, Grand Duke Mikhail, who had the political foresight to state that he would only accept the throne if invited by parliament. After the February Revolution, the royal family were kept at Tsarskoe Selo (now Pushkin) for five months with Kerensky enquiring if they had collaborated with the Germans. The British Prime Minister, David Lloyd George, offered them political asylum in Britain, but King George V would have none of it and the offer was withdrawn, thereby sealing their fate. In August 1917 they were moved to Tobolsk and in April 1918 they were taken to Ekaterinburg. When the Tsar's brother and other members of the royal family were executed by the Bolsheviks in June 1918, the future began to look bleak for Nicholas and his family. Lenin gave the go ahead to the Ekaterinburg Bolsheviks to murder them and on 17 July 1918 all were butchered in a cellar of the Ipatev house and their bodies thrown down a disused mine shaft. Boris Yeltsin, as first Party secretary of Sverdlovsk region, gave the order to destroy the house where they were killed and pave over the area, a decision he regretted later. The remains of the Tsar and his family were discovered in the mid-1970s and scientists confirmed that they were authentic in 1993. For many years a woman claimed that she was Anastasia, the youngest daughter, but after her death, scientists demonstrated that this claim was false.

Romanova, Aleksandra Fedorovna (Tsarina) (1882-1918)

She was the last, tragic, Tsarina who, despite her efforts, was never accepted at court or by the Russian people. She was a Princess of Hesse Darmstadt and her mother, Princess Alice, was a daughter of Queen Victoria. She lived in England after her mother died, when she was six, and became a favourite of Queen Victoria who called her 'sunshine'. (However she never mastered the English language and her memoirs, written in ungrammatical, unidiomatic English, have not helped her reputation.). She first travelled to Russia in 1884 where her elder sister, Elizabeth, married Grand Duke Sergei (brother of Alexander III). She met Nicholas, the heir to the throne and he later fell in love with her and they married in 1894, despite strong opposition from the Russian royal family. She converted to Orthodoxy. After four daughters, her son Aleksei was born to great rejoicing but this turned into mourning when it was discovered that he was suffering from haemophilia, an hereditary disease transmitted through the female line. Her guilt at his subsequent suffering, especially from internal bleeding, led her into mysticism. The Siberian holy man, nicknamed Rasputin, was able to staunch Aleksei's bleeding, probably by hypnosis. After the initial Russian defeats at the hands of Germans in 1914, she was seen as a German agent. This was quite unjustified but it increased her isolation. The decision of the Tsar to move to Mogilev to take over the day to day running of the war left her in charge in Petrograd. She was too easily influenced by Rasputin and acted on his suggestions, badgering her husband to make the changes she advocated. The Tsar usually took the line of least resistance and gave in. She lacked political judgement and self-confidence and when a minister contradicted her, her normal course of action was to try to have him dismissed. She was murdered, along with her husband and family, by the Bolsheviks in July 1918.

Kerensky, Aleksandr Fedorovich (1881-1970)

The great loser in twentieth-century Russian politics, Kerensky, was blamed by an army of critics for the seizure of power by the Bolsheviks in October 1917. This weighed heavily on him and until his dying day it was impossible to carry on an objective conversation with him about the events of 1917. He was liable to fly into a rage if his role was brought into question. His father was headmaster of the school in Simbirsk (Ulyanovsk) where Lenin and his elder brother Aleksandr (executed for attempted regicide in 1887) studied. He studied history and law at St Petersburg University and in 1905 joined the Social Revolutionary Party (several of his wife's relatives were in the Party). He was arrested and exiled in 1905 but returned to the capital the following year and developed into a flamboyant, silver-tongued defence lawyer. He specialised in defending political activists and travelled to Siberia to investigate the Lena gold massacre in 1912. He was elected to the Duma in 1912 as a Trudovik (socialist). Despite the boycott of the Duma by the Social Revolutionaries, Kerensky managed, not for the last time, to drive a coach and four through official Party policy. The publication of Duma (parliament) debates promoted Kerensky's name and policies and he became the most popular deputy in the eyes of workers. Like many other top politicians, he became a freemason. The February Revolution afforded him central stage and he became the most important non-Bolshevik politician in 1917. In the first Provisional Government Kerensky was Minister of Justice and when Guchkov resigned as Minister of War and the Navy, Kerensky succeeded him. This afforded him a stage for his rhetoric and he toured the fronts attempting to enthuse the troops to victory. He created a very positive image while there but it soon evaporated. The lack of clarity in his dealings with General Kornilov about suppressing Bolshevism and restoring army discipline led to Kornilov's disastrous move on Petrograd who fondly believed that he was executing Kerensky's will. This was the kiss of death for Kerensky. It confirmed Lenin's prognosis that there would be a coup from the right and any legitimacy which the Provisional Government had enjoyed in August 1917 was wiped out. He escaped arrest in the Winter Palace on 25 October 1917 by dressing up as a female nurse and attempted to rally loyal troops. He travelled to London and Paris for the Social Revolutionaries to advocate Allied intervention on the side of Russian democrats. When the Allies supported Admiral Kolchak's forces, Kerensky denounced intervention. He spent many years of his exile in Paris and, after 1940, in the United States.

Bukharin, Nikolai Ivanovich (1888-1938)

In Lenin's phrase, the 'darling of the Party', Bukharin was a sophisticated, urban intellectual who became a leading economic theorist but proved no match for Stalin. Born in Moscow, both his parents were schoolteachers, he quickly developed a taste for literature and bird and butterfly collection. He joined the Bolsheviks in 1906 and studied economics at Moscow University, 1907-10. He soon made a name for himself as a Bolshevik leader and was arrested in 1909. Imprisoned and then exiled to the Arkhangelsk region in June 1911, he managed to escape in August 1911 and remained abroad until the February Revolution. In 1913 in Vienna, at Lenin's behest, he helped Stalin (who knew no German) when the latter was writing *Marxism and the National Question.* Bukharin was often absent-minded and once, when carrying on a conversation while making soup, poured sugar instead of salt into it. He stayed in Switzerland, Norway and Sweden, before moving to New York in November 1916 and there he became an editor, alongside Trotsky, of *Novy Mir.* During his exile he wrote many of his most influential works, including one on finance capital which was heavily influenced by German Marxist thinking. He differed with Lenin on various issues, including the national question. Bukharin adopted the orthodox Marxist position that national self-determination was erroneous and potentially dangerous. He returned to Moscow, via Japan and Siberia, in May 1917 and immediately reasserted his influence among the city's Bolsheviks. He adopted a far left Bolshevik position and this led to close collaboration with Lenin. After the October Revolution he formulated Bolshevik economic policy and advocated the immediate nationalisation of industry and the building of a socialist economy. This did not please Lenin and Bukharin became a prominent Left Communist, opposing a peace treaty with Imperial Germany and instead advocated revolutionary war. However, he remained a leading member of the Bolshevik Central Committee. Bukharin came round to Lenin's views by the end of 1918 and he was as ruthless as Lenin in persecuting perceived opponents of the regime. He was elected a member of the Politburo in 1924 and chair of the Communist International (Comintern) the following year. After Lenin's death, in 1924, the strongest apparent contender for the succession was Trotsky. Bukharin entered into a tactical alliance with Stalin to vitiate the brilliant, far left firebrand. Bukharin was one of the first, if not the first, to use the expression 'socialism in one country'. This implied putting the interests of Soviet Russia ahead of world revolution. It also involved moderation at home in order to consolidate Bolshevik power. Bukharin, taking his cue from Lenin's last writings about the peasantry, viewed the road to socialism as long. Since over 80 per cent of the population were rural dwellers, agriculture would dictate the pace. Hence, the genetic or organic approach was advisable. With Trotsky ridiculing the concept of socialism in one country and advocating radical economic policies and world revolution, Bukharin and Stalin had to bide their time. Bukharin had moved far from his early extreme radicalism. As agriculture prospered, demand for industrial goods would fuel an expansion of output and the state would accumulate more taxes. The left pointed out that Soviet industry was in a sorry state and unlikely to respond to increasing demand. The question was stark: would industrialisation be achieved with the peasants as beneficiaries or at the expense of the rural sector? Whereas the left, in the works of Preobrazhensky and others, articulated their economic programme, Bukharin omitted to provide a powerful, theoretical apologia for the right wing view. The question was settled politically with Stalin the victor. Stalin then adopted, in the Five Year Plans, a more extreme version of the left's policy. Bukharin was appalled by the prospect of forced industrialisation and the concomitant authoritarian state which would automatically emerge. The nightmare of forced collectivisation was something he did not envisage. In the Gorbachev era there was considerable interest in Bukharin's views and the possibility that they represented an alternative course to Stalin's policies. Were they of value for the 1980s? We shall never know. Such was Bukharin's lack of political perception that he believed himself to be the chief beneficiary of Trotsky's defeat. Bukharin was ruthless towards the Party's opponents immediately after the revolution, but this cutting edge left him when he needed to deploy it in the intra-Party conflicts. The triumvirate of Bukharin, Rykov and Tomsky, the union of the humane and all that was best in Bolshevik socialism, was no match for the killer instincts of Stalin. Bukharin was hugely popular within the Party and this was something Stalin could not tolerate. The Politburo dumped him on 17 November 1929 and he was reduced to recanting several times in order to stay in political life. He even functioned as editor of *Izvestiya* from 1934-36. Many believe that he penned the 1936 Soviet Constitution (the most democratic in the world, in Stalin's words, and it was - at least on paper). In 1936, he was entrusted with the task of attempting to acquire archives in western Europe and met many Russian *émigrés.* He spoke frankly of his disgust and resignation about Stalin's revolution but determined to return to Moscow where he was aware he was facing imminent death. He was implicated in the Zinoviev and Kamenev show trials in 1936 and was arrested on 27 February 1937. Bakharin was the principal target of the last great show trial, in March 1938. In a whole litany of accusations, it was claimed that he had plotted to kill Lenin during the Brest-Litovsk negotiations in early 1918. After being promised that his and his young wife's life would be spared by Stalin and Voroshilov, Bukharin confessed to the most extraordinary and ludicrous (when one reads them today) crimes. He told his wife (who died recently) that he had ruined her life. He, Rykov and others were sentenced to be shot on 13 March 1938 and *Pravda* confirmed his death two days later. It was usual for prisoners to be executed immediately after their sentence by a bullet in the back of the head but it would appear that Bukharin was given a further two days' grace. His widow described him as a 'sensitive, emotional man', in Ogonek, in late 1987. His farewell letter, addressed to 'A Future Generation of Soviet Leaders', was published in *Moskovskie Novosti* (Moscow News) on 3 December 1987 and described his 'helplessness in the face of a murderous machine seeking his physical destruction'. He was rehabilitated by the USSR Supreme Soviet, together with nine others, on 4 February 1988.

Kamenev, Lev Borisovich (né Rosenfeld) (1883-1936)

The eternal moderate of the Bolshevik Party, Kamenev, was born into a Moscow Jewish family, briefly studied law at Moscow University, but discovered that being an active social democrat was more exciting. He moved to western Europe in 1907 and became a member of the Bolshevik centre, a leading Bolshevik journalist and a close collaborator of Lenin. He returned to St Petersburg in 1914 to supervise the activities of *Pravda* but was arrested the following year. After the February Revolution Kamenev situated himself on the moderate wing of the Bolshevik Party, supported co-operation with the Provisional Government and revolutionary defensism, advocated some form of fusion with the Mensheviks and accepted that the socialist revolution was a long way off, only becoming possible when capitalism had matured in Russia. Conflict with Lenin was inevitable when the Bolshevik leader managed to get back to Petrograd. When Lenin launched his April Theses - a clarion call for the taking of power by the proletariat and the poorer strata of the peasantry - Kamenev was appalled and wrote in *Pravda* that these were the personal views of comrade Lenin and not those of the Bolshevik Party. He advocated caution in the run up to the October Revolution and went so far as to publish an article in Gorky's newspaper, *Novaya Zhizn,* warning against revolutionary adventurism. This was treason - he was revealing that the Bolshevik Party was seriously contemplating seizing power - but it blew over and Lenin forgave him. Kamenev advocated a broad socialist coalition because of the narrow support base of the Bolsheviks. However, Lenin would not consider sharing power and Kamenev resigned as chair of the Central Executive Committee (CEC) of the Soviets. Lenin welcomed this as he regarded

Kamenev as too soft for the role. Instead Yakov Sverdlov, one of the hard men of the Bolshevik Party, took over and transformed the CEC, and then the Congress of Soviets into compliant bodies. Kamenev became chair of the Moscow Soviet after the revolution and remained there until ousted by Stalin. He was a leading light in the Politburo and often chaired meetings when Lenin was too ill to attend. He was Lenin's deputy as chair of Sovnarkom and chair of the council of labour and defence. As a moderate, he was always opposed to Trotsky's radicalism and he joined Stalin and Zinoviev to form the triumvirate whose aim was to prevent Trotsky succeeding Lenin, even though this was Lenin's wish. Ironically, Kamenev's wife was Trotsky's sister. Later Kamenev sided with Trotsky against Stalin and also Zinoviev in his opposition to Stalin. He lost his place on the Politburo in 1925 and was dispatched to Rome as Soviet ambassador to Italy (1926-7). He suffered the same fate as Zinoviev in being expelled several times from the Party, but readmitted when he had made the ritual obeisance to Stalin. Kamenev and Zinoviev, and a supporting cast of minor officials, had the dubious honour of starring in the first great Show Trial in Moscow in August 1936. Kamenev confessed to having been behind the murder of Sergei Kirov in 1934 and, given the opportunity, would have topped Stalin as well. All this was nonsense but Kamenev had understood that confessions would spare his own and his family's lives. They did not and the whole Kamenev household perished. Kamenev was rehabilitated under Gorbachev on 13 June 1988.

Lenin, Vladimir Ilich (1870-1924)

One of the key political actors of the twentieth century, Lenin has left an indelible mark on Russian, European and world politics. Vladimir Ilich Ulyanov adopted many pseudonyms but Lenin, probably from the River Lena in Siberia, took over in 1901. A utopian (ideas cannot be put into practice on this earth) Marxist socialist, he came to believe that will could triumph over everything else. A brilliant polemicist and tactician, Lenin had an unrivalled ability to analyse a political situation and evolve tactics to promote his Party's ends. He was better at tactical than strategic thinking but a major weakness was his inability to read the characters of his closest cohorts. He was deadly in dissecting and exploiting the weaknesses of his political opponents but he failed singularly to grasp the essence of Stalin or Trotsky. He lost his hair early and this contributed to his nickname as the 'old man' because of his seriousness and single-minded devotion to revolution. He was personally modest and hated close adulation. A member of the service nobility and a graduate in law at

St Petersburg University, he nevertheless hated the intelligentsia - they were to him the chattering classes who never moved from word to deed. Another hatred was religion - he had been religious as a teenager. In private life he could be charming among his supporters but he could be as deadly as a viper towards his enemies. He was as bloodthirsty as a vampire during the early years of the revolution but mellowed in 1921. His declining years, partly the after effects of a failed assassination attempt in August 1918 and advancing arteriosclerosis, were painful and deeply frustrating. He died a saddened and worried man.

Lenin's first contact with radical thinking was at the University of Kazan and this cost him his place. He was permitted to take his law degree (first class) as an external student at the University of St Petersburg in 1891. He practised law in Samara but moved to the capital in 1893. He soon became a professional revolutionary and visited western Europe for the first time in 1895, visiting Germany, France and Switzerland. He established contact with the Emancipation of Labour Group around Georgy Plekhanov. On his return to St Petersburg he set up a group with Yuly Martov which became known as the St Petersburg Union for Struggle for the Emancipation of the Working Class. Lenin was arrested in 1895 and exiled to Siberia from February 1897 to February 1900. During this time he wrote *The Development of Capitalism in Russia,* his first major theoretical work. He married Nadezhda Krupskaya in Siberian exile in July 1898. After completing his exile, he moved to western Europe (including Munich, London, Paris and Geneva) and, together with Martov, Plekhanov, Vera Zasulich and others, published *Iskra* (Spark), the organ of the Russian Social Democratic Workers' Party (RSDRP). In the newspaper he developed the ideas which became known as Leninism, including the concept of the professional party. When the Party split in 1903, Lenin became the leading Bolshevik, but he lost the support of Plekhanov and control of *Iskra.* He established his own newspaper, *Vpered* (Forward), but Party unity was agreed at the 1905 congress. He returned to St Petersburg in November 1905 but made little impact. He moved to Finland in 1907 and then to western Europe until the February Revolution. The experience of 1905 led him to promote the immediate transition from the bourgeois to the socialist revolution. He engaged in continuous polemics with the Mensheviks and others and in 1912 achieved one of his goals, the expulsion of the Mensheviks from the RSDRP. At the outbreak of war he moved to Bern and Zürich where he hammered away at the 'social traitors' in Russia who supported the defence of their country against Germany. He wanted Russia's defeat, believing it would promote revolution. At the Zimmerwald (1915) and Kienthal (1916) conferences in Switzerland he called for the development of the 'imperialist' war into a socialist revolution. He negotiated a deal with the German government and set off for Petrograd in March 1917 in the famous 'sealed train' (the doors were sealed). On his arrival in Petrograd on 4 April, he proclaimed the April Theses (see page 60), one of the key political documents of the era. It is a major contribution to Marxism-Leninism. He called for the transition from the first stage of the revolution to the second, the socialist stage, immediately. Russia would be administered by soviets and implacable hostility was to be shown the Provisional Government. Few supported him at the time but the Bolsheviks grew until they had the majority in the St Petersburg Soviet by September. After the July Days Lenin had to disguise himself as a mute Finnish railway fireman (he knew no Finnish) to move to Finland. He continued to urge insurrection (Lenin never referred to the events of October as a revolution) and eventually the Central Committee agreed. Trotsky's view that the opening of the 2nd Congress of Soviets on 25 October 1917 should be the moment for the declaration of Soviet power, was accepted. The Bolshevik take-over was therefore a soviet revolution which ushered in a Soviet Russia. Lenin became chair of Sovnarkom and developed a passion for governmental detail. He never occupied a top Party post but was the acknowledged leader. He insisted that a peace treaty be signed with Germany and eventually he had his way but it led to the attempt on his life, in August 1918. He was honest enough in 1921 to admit that the industrial proletariat had ceased to exist. The tactical retreat of the New Economic Policy in 1921 revealed that he had lost none of his political guile. His flawed legacy was only recognised by the communists in the late Gorbachev era.

Trotsky, Lev Davidovich (né Bronstein) (1879-1940)

The most gifted orator and writer among the Bolsheviks, he was second only to Lenin in October 1917 and afterwards, but the leader's illness from 1922 onwards also marks Trotsky's political demise. He was a great bridesmaid but was quite incapable politically of ever becoming the bride. Perhaps it was due to his Jewishness that a gulf opened up between himself and ordinary people. He singularly failed to build up his own political 'tail', despite widespread support for his left communist views. A comrade once remarked that one could understand everything that Stalin said, some of what Lenin was saying, but Trotsky, he was talking to the gods. He is the classic case of the intellectual in politics who is easily outmanoeuvred by the more mundane Party machine man. His prose is the most brilliant of the revolution but only a small minority were educated. A talented organiser, he threw himself with immense energy into tasks which interested him, but these were followed by periods of lassitude. Stalin hated and feared him and relentlessly attempted to denigrate him in the eyes of Lenin. This gradually affected Trotsky's health - one is tempted to say that many of his post-1922 illnesses were psychosomatic - and he needed to take time off to recuperate in the south. His wife comments that on one occasion, after a tempestuous Party meeting, he returned home bathed in sweat. It was remarkable that Trotsky subordinated himself to Lenin after August 1917 since earlier there had been many bitter feuds with the Bolshevik leader. Trotsky always saw himself as a natural number one, never as a number two. He first met Lenin in London in 1902 and there was mutual respect but at the 2nd RSDRP Congress in 1903 he violently criticised Lenin's organisational blueprint for the Party, regarding him as a dictator and reminiscent of the mad Robespierre, the tyrant of the French Revolution. Trotsky was also ill-suited to the moderate views of the Mensheviks but in 1905 he was a leading figure in the St Petersburg Soviet. He alternated between arrest, exile and escape but eventually moved abroad and travelled widely, participating everywhere in social democratic affairs. He was in New York when the February Revolution broke out and got back to Petrograd in May 1917. He merged his own group, Mezhraionka, with the Bolshevik Party and set sail under Bolshevik colours. One reason why he was reconciled with Lenin was that the latter had adopted Trotsky's theory of permanent revolution. Trotsky, like Lenin, scented revolution in the air in the summer of 1917. As head of the Military Revolutionary Committee, the General Staff of the revolution, in Petrograd, Trotsky played a vital role in the Bolshevik success. He was Commissar for Foreign Affairs in the first Sovnarkom (he saw himself as the conductor of world revolution) and given the distasteful job of negotiating a peace treaty with the Germans and Austrians. Convinced that revolution in Germany was imminent, Trotsky dragged out proceedings (had the Bolsheviks concluded peace in late 1917 they would have obtained much better terms than in March 1918), always expecting a telegram informing that Berlin was red. The peace issue tore the Party apart. Lenin wanted peace at any price and Bukharin and the left communists would not conclude peace at any price. Trotsky, typically, came up with the slogan of neither peace nor war, based on the false premise that the Germans were militarily incapable of advancing on the Russian front. He departed the foreign affairs scene in March 1918 and was appointed Commissar for War and president of the Supreme War Council. He organised the Red Army from scratch and mastered military theory on the hoof. This was a brilliant achievement and he played the key role in ensuring that the Bolshevik regime survived. During the Civil War he clashed repeatedly with Stalin. It later became clear to Lenin that the two comrades could not stand one another and this could have disastrous consequences for the Party. Lenin regarded Trotsky as his natural successor but declined to propose this to the Party. This permitted the others to organise against Trotsky. It was almost child's play to outmanoeuvre Trotsky and the master manipulator was Stalin. No Bolshevik saw Stalin's end game which was to become leader. Trotsky sided with the left in economics and advocated aid to revolutionary movements outside Russia. Stalin, sensing the mood of the country, put the security of the revolution in Russia ahead of international adventures. He, therefore, supported socialism in one country, which Trotsky ridiculed. Trotsky resigned his last important state office, Commissar for War, in 1925, when he could have hung on. Trotsky had been one of the builders of the Party which permitted the leaders to silence their critics and, in desperation, he and his supporters took to the streets, in November 1927, to publicise their opposition to Stalin and his policies. He was exiled in 1928 and eventually went abroad, surprisingly being allowed by Stalin to take his archive with him, and eventually found refuge in Mexico in 1937. He continued his bitter feud with Stalin but by now it was David against Goliath. Despite this Stalin was always nervous about Trotsky's potential influence and his political police attempted to murder Trotsky on several occasions. They eventually succeeded in August 1940. Trotsky's writings inspired a legion of disciples, especially in the universities of the capitalist world, but their influence waned after the 1970s.

Stalin, Iosif Vissarionovich (né Dzhugashvili) (1979-1953)

He is one of the dominant political actors of the twentieth century who has left an indelible mark on Russia and the world. The system he spawned, Stalinism, lived after him. Short of stature, with a pock-marked face, Stalin did not speak Russian until the age of 11. A Georgian by birth (his father was of Ossetian origin, the family name is Ossetian with a Georgian suffix), he came to dominate Soviet Russia in a manner that no communist leader had done before or after him. He both craved for, and was repelled by, personal adulation. A French diplomat exclaimed, *Mon Dieu* (My God), on beholding a huge portrait of Stalin being trailed across the sky. 'Precisely, monsieur', replied his companion. The Stalin cult was presenting Stalin as a god. He had slightly yellow eyes and could silence any Soviet general or politician by merely fixing them on him. He was very well read, possessed of an elephantine memory and never forgot a slight. He was highly intelligent and had a great facility to grasp an argument, draft memoranda and penetrate to the core of any matter. His Russian prose is clear and fluent and bears testimony to his days in a Georgian Orthodox seminary where he was being trained as a priest. He was a master of intrigue and a shrewd tactician. He was a Hercules Poirot when it came to detecting the human weaknesses of an opponent. Stalin then ruthlessly and mercilessly exploited his advantage. Trotsky, intellectually more gifted was, nevertheless, like a rabbit being mesmerised by Stalin the stoat. He acted according to the maxim: if in doubt, never trust anyone. However, he did trust Hitler, for some unfathomable reason, and lived to regret it. He never made the mistake of trusting a foreign politician again.

Lenin early identified Stalin as a coming comrade and he was elected to the Central Committee of the RSDRP in 1912. He was a professional revolutionary and, among other things, robbed banks to augment Party finances. He was a delegate to several Party Congresses. The following year, Lenin commissioned Stalin to write an extended essay on Marxism and the nationality question, a subject of increasing significance at that time. He spent a month in Vienna composing the work, with Bukharin helping him since he knew no German. He was exiled to north Siberia in 1913 (Sverdlov was a fellow comrade but they did not get on) and the February Revolution liberated him. He immediately returned to Petrograd and, after Lenin's return, adopted Lenin's position and became one of his closest collaborators. Lenin made him Commissar for Nationalities (until 1923) in the first Sovnarkom and hence became, with Lenin, responsible for policy towards non-Russians. He was deeply involved in military-political affairs during the Civil War and the first serious conflicts with Trotsky date from this period. Stalin used his activities to develop his network of friends and subordinates. He was made general secretary of the Party in 1922 but no one at that time regarded the post as important. Stalin, as a member of the Politburo, Central Committee and Organisational Bureau (Orgburo), was the best informed comrade in the Party. His relations with Krupskaya, Lenin's wife, reached such a nadir that Lenin proposed in late 1922, in his Testament, that Stalin be shorn of his position as Party general secretary. At Lenin's funeral he delivered a quasi-religious eulogy to the dead leader and thereafter claimed to be Lenin's chief pupil. His skill at coalition politics produced victories over the left-leaning Trotsky, Kamenev, Zinoviev and, finally, the right-leaning Bukharin. This made Stalin the main political actor but Stalinism did not really take root until 1936. It can be defined as concentrating the decision-making process at the centre, mobilising the resources of the country and giving preference to defence-related heavy industries, eliminating the market mechanism, transforming education and culture into weapons in the great struggle to become the leading world power. Everyone and everything should serve the economic goals of the state. The phenomenon was dominated by the cult of Stalin's personality. Extraordinary economic feats were recorded but at an appalling human cost - of no importance to Stalin. He decided that a pact with Germany would keep the USSR out of the coming European war and appears to have sought agreement with Hitler from 1936. The German invasion of June 1941 stunned him and Molotov made the announcement of the attack to the Soviet people. Stalin was very vulnerable and could have been removed but his comrades decided that he was an asset not a liability. It took him about two years to learn mechanised warfare but he became a popular and astute war leader. The wartime conferences with the Allies made him very popular in the West (he was known as Uncle Joe and it had to be explained to him that this was an affectionate nickname). The

Russians acquired another empire after 1945, in eastern and south-eastern Europe, and the rule was that the Party set up shop after the Red Army had finished its work. Stalin did not want Mao Zedong and the communists to take power in China until he had established some sort of control over them. When Mao came to Moscow in 1950 to request aid Stalin attempted to humiliate him, eventually providing some aid but charged interest. However, to counterbalance this, Stalin revealed to Mao the names of the Chinese comrades working for him. Mao quickly liquidated them. Stalin fell out with Tito, the Yugoslav leader, in 1948 because he thought him too independent. Stalin failed to develop good relations with the West after 1945 and the Cold War took hold in 1947. This began an arms race which eventually proved a great economic liability for Moscow. Stalin's declining years saw him withdraw from the public gaze and become erratic and, indeed, paranoid. One of his doctors advised him to retire but Stalin characteristically turned on him. His death was slow and painful. It was his custom to lock himself in his quarters for the night. He suffered a stroke during the night and was only found in the morning. There was still a record on the gramophone. Stalin had spent his last hours listening to Chopin, played by a Russian pianist.

Zinoviev, Grigory Evseevich (né Radomyslsky) (1883-1936)

In Trotsky's memorable phrase, Zinoviev was either in seventh heaven or in the depths of despair. A volatile politician, a passionate orator, he proved no match for the master game player, Stalin. His Jewish family owned a dairy farm. He joined the RSDRP in 1901. He moved abroad and met Lenin and Plekhanov in 1903 and, after the Party split, sided with Lenin, remaining close to him in exile until 1917. He was in St Petersburg during the 1905 revolution and was elected to the Central Committee of the RSDRP in 1907. He became editor of Lenin's publications in exile and passed the war in Switzerland, returning with him and others to Petrograd in April 1917. He went into hiding with Lenin in Finland after the July Days but, together with Kamenev, he opposed the Bolshevik armed uprising in October. They published an article to this effect in *Novaya Zhizn,* and this threatened to derail the uprising. Fortunately for the Bolsheviks, Kerensky laughed it off by saying that had the Bolsheviks been planning an insurrection they would hardly announce it beforehand in the press. After the October Revolution Zinoviev favoured the formation of a broad socialist coalition government and opposed Lenin's insistence on a Bolshevik government. He and four others resigned from the Central Committee in protest but were quickly readmitted. He was elected chair of the executive committee of the Communist International (Comintern) at its first congress in 1919. During the Kronstadt uprising Trotsky found him in a panic and he was saved by Trotsky and (later Marshal) Tukhachevsky. Stalin drew him and Kamenev into a tactical alliance against Trotsky after

Lenin's death but after Trotsky's defeat Stalin turned on his erstwhile allies. In 1926 Zinoviev lost his place on the Politburo and his Comintern post and was expelled from the Party in November 1927 after going on to the streets, with Trotsky and others, to protest vainly against Stalin's policies. He was readmitted to the Party in 1928 after recanting his views and praising Stalin to the skies. He was expelled again in 1932. He (and Kamenev) were tried in secret in January 1935 and he was sentenced to 10 years' imprisonment. In April 1936 he was the main defendant in the first Show Trial. He cut a pathetic figure but abject submission did not save him from the executioner's bullet. As an Old Bolshevik (those who had joined the Party before 1917) he was a marked man as far as Stalin was concerned. He was rehabilitated under Gorbachev.

The Church, Tsardom and the bourgeoisie cast off by the Russian people. A cartoon from 1919

4 The 1917 Revolutions and the Civil War

Petrograd, The February 1917 Revolution

The Tsar's government had prepared to deal with disorder and increased the number of police and troops in the capital, Petrograd, in early 1917. Despite this, and despite the fact that in February there was no planning for revolution as there was to be in October, Tsarism was swept away because it had too few supporters.

From early February there were street demonstrations in Petrograd. The demonstrators wanted more bread and the workers, hit by inflation, wanted more pay. By 23 February, some of the 90,000 workers who were on strike joined the demonstrations but the streets were cleared by the police and troops. The next day, 24 February, some 200,000 workers were on strike, the demonstrators moved to the centre of Petrograd and there were signs of sympathy between the demonstrators and the troops. On 25 February, the Tsar sent a telegram to the commander of the Petrograd garrison 'I command you to suppress ... all disorders on the streets of the capital ... '. This was done and about 80 demonstrators were killed but from that day mutinies among the troops began. Rodzyanko, the President of the Duma, wrote on 26 February 'There is anarchy in the capital. The government is paralysed. It is necessary immediately to entrust a person who enjoys the confidence of the country with the formation of a new government. There must be no delay.' The next day, the Tsar's power in Petrograd having slipped away like life from a dying man, the Duma elected an executive committee and took on the governing of Russia. For further details of these events please see the Chronology, pages 12-15.

February 1917: the Unexpected Revolution

In February 1917 no one expected the monarchy to collapse, thus giving birth to revolution. The ever optimist Lenin was rather pessimistic in January 1917 and spoke of not living to see the revolution. The Mensheviks thought that revolution would come about but that it would be the bourgeoisie, the middle classes, who would overcome the Tsar and take control of the country. This could mean the end of the monarchy or the evolution of a constitutional monarchy. The Mensheviks were looking forward to the next revolution, one which would see power passing to the working class. However, that could only occur when Russia was a developed industrial state. The SRs (Social Revolutionaries, glossary page 119 and pages 29-30) devoted much of their energies after 1914 to the war effort, or rather criticising the incompetent Tsarist running of the war.

Reasons for the Victory of the February Revolution

- The most important reason was that the forces of coercion, the army and the police, changed sides. No ruling class can stay in power if the men and women with guns refuse to obey and defend it.

  By 1917 Nicholas II had alienated almost everyone by his poor leadership and indecisiveness. Read the biographical sketch on pages 40-1.
- The Tsar was in Mogilev not in his capital, Petrograd. Hence he had to give orders - they were always the same - use force - from a distance without being able to judge for himself the seriousness of the situation.
- The army was a defeated army and was no match for the Germans. However, it fared much better against the Austrians and the Turks. This was irrelevant since the Germans were threatening Petrograd and the low morale of the armies confronting the Germans was decisive.
- Bolshevik propaganda among the front line troops and those in the rear was quite effective. They advocated an immediate peace and stated that the war was imperialist, being fought only in the interests of the ruling classes of Russia and Germany.
- The Tsarist administration completely failed to convince Russian soldiers that a German victory could mean that Russia would become a German colony. Compare the way the Russians fought the Germans in 1914-17 - badly - to the way they fought in 1941-5 when everyone believed that he was fighting for his life as a Nazi victory meant slavery or extermination.
- The Tsarist regime did not understand the urgency of efficient management of the war. It began by thinking that the war would be short - less than six months - but as the war dragged on it did not respond by setting up new institutions to administer the war. One reason for this was the personnel involved, the Tsar and the nobility wanted to keep control of the country. These men were incapable of running a modern state, let alone one facing a terrible war. The business class wanted to participate and set up the War Industries Committee but the establishment resented their interference. The new problems posed by the war required a pooling of all the talents in the country but the Tsar held back from this because of his fear of losing control. This underlined his lack of intellectual self-confidence.
- The Duma deputies refused to disband as the Tsar ordered and this was very significant - most of the deputies were from the then ruling and upper classes. The Tsar had few supporters left.

- Duma deputies advised the Tsar to abdicate but the military and members of his own family and court did the same.
- The officer corps became less and less committed to the Tsar as its numbers were decimated and new fresh blood was brought in from other parts of society. Many of these young men did not want to be officers and often feared their own men.
- Food shortages were important. Grain production during the first two years of the war was about 10 per cent above the average of the 1909-13 period. However, in 1916 and 1917 production fell. In 1917 it was a quarter less than in 1915. This did not really matter as grain was not being exported, which meant that more was available for home consumption. A major factor was the creation of a huge army, 15.1 million men had been mobilised by mid-1917, over one-third of males of working age. In 1914 and 1915 the army was well catered for but in 1916 and 1917 there were serious shortfalls. In March 1917 the bread ration was down to 1.8lb per day, compared to 2.7lb in 1916. There was enough food in the country to feed the army and the rest of the population but transport bottlenecks meant that it could not be moved to the areas which needed it most. Petrograd suffered greater shortages than Moscow. Communications, or the lack of them, was an important contributory factor to creating the conditions which produced the February Revolution in Petrograd.
- Culturally there was a mood of revolution which pervaded literature, music, art and so on. The intelligentsia came to believe that revolution could only bring good.

What the Main Political Parties and Groups Expected of the February Revolution and What Would Happen Next

- The Octobrists and Kadets who dominated the first Provisional Government (2 March 1917) issued a statement about the work of the cabinet. They stated that there would be an immediate amnesty of all convicted for political and religious offences, terrorism, military and rural revolts. There would be freedom of speech and assembly, the right to form unions and to strike. All restrictions based on class, religion and nationality were abolished. A Constituent Assembly (parliament) was to be elected on the basis of universal, equal and direct suffrage. The police were to be replaced by a militia, with officers elected and subject to local government control. There were to be elections to organs of local self-government. The military units which participated in the revolutionary movement were not to be disbanded or removed from Petrograd. Soldiers were to be subject to strict military discipline on duty and during military service but to enjoy those civil rights which all other citizens possess. This was a remarkably radical programme for conservatives but less so for the liberals.

The Octobrists hoped that the business class would have the dominant say in government and that their wealth could be protected and grow. The Kadets wanted a constitutional state (some of them would have preferred a constitutional monarchy since a Tsar would have stood for authority and a flourishing market economy. Both parties wanted to stay in the war until it was won.

- The SRs promised to be the strongest party in Russia, given one man, one woman, one vote. Since their main support base was among the peasantry, they advocated the transfer of land held by the ruling and upper classes to the rural dwellers. Who was to decide who got what and if compensation was to be paid? That was to be left to the Constituent Assembly (CA) the SRs would be in the majority. The SRs did not think that they should participate in the first Provisional Government since they accepted that the revolution was bourgeois, the middle classes had the right to rule. The CA would draft a constitution and appoint a government. They could then decide which portfolios to accept.
- The Mensheviks, like the SRs, accepted that the middle classes had the right to take the lead after February. As Marxists they did not wish to participate in a bourgeois government. Following the lead of the German social democrats (SPD), they believed that the socialist revolution could only occur successfully when a country was highly developed industrially. During the capitalist stage of development, they would learn democracy and acquire the skills of running the state when they took over. They did not fear the bourgeoisie, they feared reaction from the right and the military.
- The Bolsheviks in February agreed with the Mensheviks, that is, those Bolsheviks who were in Petrograd at the time or returned just afterwards. These included Molotov and Stalin. The comrade who changed everything was Lenin. He perceived that the state after February was weak because it could not rely on the armed forces or the police. He took on board Trotsky's concept of permanent revolution, this is that the bourgeois revolution could lead in a relatively short time to a socialist revolution, where the working class would have power. In line with this, on his return to Petrograd on 4 April, he launched his April Theses or proposals. They constitute one of the most important documents of the twentieth century. He advocated hostility to the Provisional Government, the transition from the first stage of the revolution to the second, worker power, all power to the soviets - Russia was to become a land of the soviets, all landed estates were to be confiscated without compensation and all land nationalised and the Party was to change its name. This immediately split the Bolshevik Party with Kamenev and Zinoviev writing in *Pravda* that Lenin did not

speak for the Party, merely for himself. Clearly Lenin had a formidable task ahead of him if he was going to win over the Party leadership to his radical views on revolution.

- Ukraine expected autonomy within the new state and the right to develop its own language, culture and economy.
- Finland and Poland expected independence from Russia.
- The non-Russian nationalities expected greater autonomy within the new state or to become independent. They demanded the right of national self-determination. The Muslims wanted to develop their own territory and become part of the world Islamic umaa.

The Key Turning Points of the Period February-October 1917

- Order No. 1, issued by the Petrograd Soviet and published in its newspaper, *Izvestiya* (news in Russian), on 2 March 1917, the same day as the first Provisional Government took office, transformed relations between officers and men in the military. It stated that committees were to be elected in all companies, battalions, etc and in all naval vessels from the rank and file; that all troop units which had not yet elected their representatives to the Petrograd Soviet were to elect one per company; in all political actions, troops are subordinate to the Petrograd Soviet; the orders of the military commission of the State Duma are to be obeyed in so far as they do not contradict the orders and decrees of the Petrograd Soviet; all arms are to be placed under the control of company and battalion committees and not to be issued to officers, even upon demand; on duty soldiers shall observe military discipline but when off duty they enjoy the rights of other citizens. This order effectively placed the military under the Petrograd Soviet and undermined from the very beginning the power of the Provisional Government. Hence, dual authority or dual power (the Provisional Government and the Petrograd Soviet) was established immediately after the victory of the February Revolution.
- The arrival of Lenin and the proclamation of his April Theses transformed the political situation. Whereas the Provisional Government only had enemies on the right, it now had enemies on the left.
- The determination of the Provisional Government to honour the previous regime's war obligations to the allies led to Milyukov's note of 18 April mentioning sanctions and guarantees to be sought. This was like a red rag to a bull as soldiers regarded the February Revolution as effectively ending the war. The demonstrations brought down the government and led to the appointment of the first coalition government of 5 May.
- The moderate socialists (SRs and Mensheviks) who dominated the Petrograd Soviet decided to join the bourgeois government because of

its weakness and fear of the right. This then made the moderate socialists responsible for all the grievances of the period. It was also a gift to the Bolsheviks who could now claim that the Mensheviks had sold out to the bourgeoisie and that only they represented the interests of the workers.

- The Bolsheviks promoted the slogan of all power to the soviets and, by extension, the overthrow of the Provisional Government. They continually held demonstrations to promote this message and in early June the Petrograd Soviet banned a Bolshevik demonstration fearing bloodshed.
- The Allied offensive in the west in June 1917 led to requests that Russia launch an offensive on the eastern front. This became known as the Kerensky offensive and resulted in disaster. The Bolsheviks seized this opportunity and sailors from the naval base of Kronstadt poured into Petrograd on 3 and 4 July and helped swell the huge demonstrations, opposed by the Petrograd Soviet. Viktor Chernov, the SR Minister of Agriculture, was almost lynched, as the crowd demanded that the Soviet take power. Eventually the Bolsheviks backed down and obeyed a Petrograd Soviet appeal to call off the protests. However, it was a near run thing and made very clear the rising tide of Bolshevik support. It also revealed that the Bolsheviks had few political allies.
- Trotsky's decision to side with Lenin provides him with a formidable ally.
- The Provisional Government's action against *Pravda* and leading Bolsheviks polarised the political situation and was not decisive enough to neutralise the Bolshevik threat. The failure to arrest Lenin is important as he escapes to Finland and plots the seizure of power from there.
- In the April Theses (see page 60) Lenin had called for the nationalisation of all land, including that of the peasants, and the setting up of model farms on confiscated landed estates. The peasants paid no attention to this and carried on seizing land as they needed more land to produce more food to survive. Lenin came to see the poor peasants as the strategic allies of the workers. There was also the fact that most soldiers were peasants in uniform and found Lenin's calls for an immediate peace attractive. As a Marxist, Lenin could not advocate that the seized land should become the private property of the peasants, he was not in the business of promoting a property-owning bourgeois state. However, he came to realise that, in the short term, the Bolsheviks had much to gain from the actions of the peasants in the countryside since they were stripping the rural bourgeoisie of their wealth. A policy of immediate peace would paralyse the army as soldiers made their way home and a policy of land to the peasants

Document: Lenin's April Theses

1. In our attitude to the war not the slightest concession must be made to 'revolutionary defensism', for even under the new government of Lvov and Co the war on Russia's part unquestionably remains a predatory imperialist war owing to the capitalist nature of that government …

2. The specific feature of the present situation in Russia is that it represents a transition from the first stage of the revolution - which, owing to the insufficient class consciousness and organisation of the proletariat, led to the assumption of power by the bourgeoisie - to the second stage, which must place power in the hands of the proletariat and the poor strata of the peasantry …

3. No support must be given the Provisional Government …

4. … It must be explained to the masses that the Soviets of Workers' Deputies is the only possible form of revolutionary government …

5. Not a parliamentary republic - but a republic of Soviets of Workers', Agricultural Labourers' and Peasants' Deputies throughout the country, from top to bottom. Abolition of the police, army and the bureaucracy …

6. … Confiscation of all landed estates. Nationalisation of all land in the country, the disposal of such lands to be in the charge of the local Soviets of Agricultural Labourers' and Peasants' Deputies. The organisation of separate Soviets of Poor Peasants …

8. Our immediate task shall not be the 'introduction of socialism', but to bring social production and distribution of products only under the control of the Soviets of Workers' Deputies.

9. … A new name for the Party …

10. A new International …

---

would accelerate the move from the front to the home villages. It did not matter that the slogan of land to the peasants was SR policy. Lenin boldly stated that he was in favour of its implementation now. This move split the SR Party into right SRs, who argued that only the Constituent Assembly could decide the land question, and the left SRs, who sided with the Bolsheviks on this and every other major issue until October.

- Kerensky was a ditherer, a silver-tongued lawyer who courted popularity but was unable to take harsh, decisive decisions when the occasion demanded. He was aware that there was danger on the left from the Bolsheviks but did not believe they could take power or, if they did, they would not last long. He always headed weak, coalition governments and found that his ministers would not sanction any really coercive action against political opponents or the army. The Mensheviks, the Social Democrats, disappointed him as they waited on events rather than trying to shape them. This was mainly because they were uncomfortable in an alliance with bourgeois parties. They also regarded violence against fellow Social Democrats, the Bolsheviks, as inadmissible. See Kerensky's biography on pages 42-3.
- The misunderstanding between Kerensky and Kornilov leads to

Kornilov attempting to march on Petrograd and arrest the Soviet. This confirms Lenin's analysis, immediately after the July Days, that an imminent coup from the right can be expected. The failure of the move demonstrates that the military are not under the control of the Provisional Government.

- In calling for the defence of Petrograd, the government issues arms which are not returned when Kornilov is defeated. The Petrograd Soviet now has the arms to seize power if and when desired.
- The Military Revolutionary Committee (MRC) of the Petrograd Soviet, chaired by Trotsky, provides the Bolsheviks with the opportunity of organising behind the façade of the Petrograd Soviet.
- Rising inflation and shortages made life increasing difficult for the urban population and by September the Bolsheviks are in the majority in the Petrograd and Moscow Soviets.
- The key variable in the situation between February and October is Lenin. The April Theses provide a blueprint for action but he was too radical for most Bolsheviks until October. The majority of Bolsheviks were afraid of risking an uprising lest it result in failure and probably their deaths as the Provisional Government took revenge. It is still unclear if Lenin wanted the Soviets to take power from the Provisional Government during the July Days. If not, it revels his tactical grasp of the situation - the risk of failure was too high as events were too spontaneous. In September he advocates the seizure of power but he is not yet in the majority in the Bolshevik leadership. Then, gradually, he wins over the majority (Kamenev and Zinoviev resisted to the end). Trotsky was as radical as Lenin and was an important ally. Stalin tends to hedge his bets but supports Lenin in key decisions. During this period Lenin was not acknowledged as the sole leader of the Bolshevik Party but he was *primus inter pares* (first among equals). Hence, others could and did challenge his decisions.

The Provisional Government

A few changes were made immediately by the Provisional Government. Political prisoners were released, secret courts ended and the press liberalised. Apart from a decree for an eight-hour day, nothing was done for working people and peasants, who wanted land, gained only a committee to consider land reform.

The greatest feature of the government was inactivity, while elections were planned for a Constitutional Assembly (which met in January 1918, for one day, before it was dismissed by Lenin). Most damaging for their support was the Provisional Government's continuation of the war, notably the Kerensky offensive of June-July. Its failure led to further food shortages and inflation and demonstrations by workers, soldiers and sailors on

3-4 July. Troops were used to suppress the demonstrators. Some Bolsheviks, who were blamed for the unrest, were arrested. From 25 July, opponents of the Provisional Government, led by Commander in Chief Kornilov, attempted to occupy Petrograd, but the Soviets, supported by the Bolshevik Red Guard, prevented this.

It is important to note that within hours of the setting up of the Provisional Government a Soviet (Soldiers' and Workers' Council) was set up in the Tauride Palace as a parallel and rival power to the Provisional Government. Petrograd was under the influence of the Soviets.

Why the Provisional Government Failed

- Everything it did was provisional or temporary, hence strong, decisive government is absent.
- Order No. 1 removed control of the military from it and it also had little control over the police.
- The Provisional Government shared power with the Petrograd Soviet from the very beginning: hence there was dual power.
- The Provisional Government never produced a decisive leader of the calibre of Lenin.
- The decision to continue the war was rejected by the vast majority of the army and the population.
- Land seizures accelerated when peasants found that the government lacked the willpower to prevent them.
- Inflation from mid-1917 destroyed government economic policy.
- Kerensky underestimated Lenin and the Bolsheviks and when Kamenev and Zinoviev, in the press, stated that they opposed the coming Bolshevik uprising, Kerensky took to his couch in laughter.
- The Mensheviks were opposed to violence and did not believe that the Bolsheviks would use it, even if they did seize power. They always defended Lenin against claims by the right that he was violent.
- Lenin's brilliant political tactics and leadership.

The October Revolution

If the February Revolution was a haphazard affair, without any central direction, the October Revolution was quite different. It was planned and executed like a game of chess. Lenin and Trotsky had the nerve to go for power knowing that they were taking a tremendous risk but there was no way they could guarantee success. The decision to take power and present it to the 2nd Congress of Soviets was very astute. It was not a Bolshevik seizure of power but a soviet revolution. Arguably, the majority of Russian citizens supported the revolution. It appeared to give power to the workers, land to the peasants, national self-determination to non-Russians and an end to the war. If a majority of people support a revolution it becomes democratic. What they did not support was the Bolsheviks ruling on their own: socialists expected a coalition government, a coalition of all socialist parties. The first Sovnarkom government, headed by Lenin, was all-Bolshevik and, after protests a coalition government, including a few left SRs in not very important posts, did take office in December 1917 but melted away in March 1918 after the treaty of Brest-Litovsk. After that only communists held office and it was not until the Gorbachev era that non-communists could occupy significant positions in government.

The Institutions the Bolsheviks Created to Rule Soviet Russia

The Communist Party. Only a member of the Party was referred to as a communist so, technically, a small percentage of the population was communist. The Communist Party was run according to the principles of democratic centralism. This meant that those below always carried out the orders of those above and that local committees were answerable to those above and they, in turn, supervised those below. The basic organisation, the cell, could consist of only a few comrades - communists addressed one another as comrade (*tovarishch* in Russian). The title *gospodin* or Mr is out of fashion after October 1917. Each factory, school, etc has its Party committee. Each *raion* (district) of a city has a Party committee, all subordinate to the city Party committee. All *oblasts* or *krais* (provinces) also have their own Party committees as does each republic. The head of a committee is called a first secretary and only at the *raion, oblast/krai* and republican level is he (very rarely she) a full time, paid official. Each republican Party elects a Central Committee and a Central Revision Committee (CCC) (responsible for supervising the behaviour of Party members). The Party appears to be a federal Party, consisting of all the republican Parties, all making up a Soviet Party. In reality the Party was always centralised with Moscow dictating policy. At the centre there is a Politburo which is the key policy-making body. Before February 1917 the Bolsheviks were a conspiratorial party and hence when they took power they had to set up a network which spanned the country. This was a formidable undertaking, given that the Bolsheviks were a minority in the state. A major problem they faced was that many joined for career purposes and knew little and cared less about the finer points of Marxist socialism. Periodic purges of the Party is the weapon used to cleanse it from time to time.

Sovnarkom, the government. Like any other state, Soviet Russia needed a government to run it. It is interesting that the ministries (commissariats) of the Soviet government were almost exactly the same as those of the Tsarist government. Lenin chose to be head of government and was fascinated by administrative detail. He found it very difficult to delegate and so everyone appealed to him as a court of last resort. He was asked once to decide on the ownership of a bicycle!

The pillars of the soviet regime: Krylenko, the Procurator General of the Republic. (The words on the buildings are 'Mortury' and 'Crematory' - Krylenko sentenced so many to death.)

The soviets. These were local government bodies and the supreme elective organs of the state. There were soviets everywhere: it was the in thing for any group to set up a soviet, and the top of the tree was the Congress of Soviets and its executive committee. The soviets were responsible for most legislation but the CC could also pass decrees and instructions which had the force of law.

The Relationship Between the Institutions of the Soviet State

What was the relationship between these institutions? Which one took precedence? This was never officially laid down. In reality immediately after October many Bolsheviks headed for the soviets so as to implement soviet power and also, of course, to attempt to enforce Bolshevik control. The conflict over the treaty of Brest-Litovsk demonstrated to Lenin the unreliability of the soviets (meaning that they opposed him). Conflict over whether there should be a coalition government or not weakened Sovnarkom as did Lenin's decision to allow commissars who lost an argument over policy in Sovnarkom to appeal to the Politburo. The onset of the Civil War in the summer of 1918 increased pressure on the Bolsheviks and they became increasingly dictatorial in order to survive. Gradually the Politburo became the leading institution and this was quite clear by 1921. Hence, in October 1917, the soviets were first, the government second and the Party third, but in 1921 the Party was first, the government second and the soviets third. This was an important reason why democracy did not develop in Russia (democracy being understood as a plurality of views).

There are two other influential institutions which kept the Bolsheviks in power: First, the Cheka or political police (later called the GPU, the OGPU, the NKVD, the MVD, the MGB and the KGB), set up in December 1917 to defend Bolshevik power. It developed the reputation of being a deadly organisation (the number of corpses can be counted in thousands, later millions) and its brief was to eliminate anyone opposing the regime. Eventually this came to include communists as well. Second, the Peasants and Workers' Red Army, founded in February 1918, to defend the country against the Germans, it learnt its trade during the Civil War (1918-20).

Economic Policy, October 1917-29

Lenin did not want to introduce socialism after October (nationalisation of the factories, land, trade and banking managed by the workers) since he did not believe workers had the expertise to run an economy. Bolshevik economic policy went through three stages by 1921:

- *State capitalism:* October 1917-June 1918. Lenin and Trotsky favoured the continuation of the capitalist economy with workers supervising management.

- *War communism:* June 1918-March 1921. Lenin and the Bolsheviks were greatly impressed by the German war economy which centralised all decisions and labour was not permitted to move without permission. He coined the expression integral socialism to describe his understanding of the future socialist economy. It would be a combination of the German military economic machine ('here we have the last word in modern large scale capitalist technology and planned organisation') with Soviet power. The future socialist economy would have tightly controlled production and distribution with strict norms of consumption and exchange in kind. War communism rejected personal interest as 'petty bourgeois' and the worker was conceived of as a bolt in a machine. Initially, the Bolsheviks attempted to manage the economy centrally through labour organisations (factory committees, trade unions, soviets, etc) but it soon turned out that workers' control promoted local and consumer interests rather than efficiency, accumulation and economic growth. Then the Bolsheviks attempted to fashion a Supreme Council of the National Economy (VSNKh) to manage all enterprises in the country and eventually the whole economy. Nationalisation of enterprises was accelerated very rapidly. The view was that VSNKh would bring enterprises together and manage them as parts of a single factory. The market economy was to be superseded by planning. Inflation was very high and destroyed paper money with many going over to barter (exchange of goods without any money changing hands). VSNKh also proved ineffective in managing the economy under civil war conditions and so unpopular was war communism that it almost brought the Bolsheviks down.
- *The New Economic Policy* (NEP): March 1921-1929. Revolts by peasants in Tambov and elsewhere, refusing to deliver food to the state because they regarded state requisitioning as extortion, led to a U-turn by Lenin. Victory in the Civil War allowed the Bolsheviks to relax the reins and impose their authority throughout the country. Industry and agriculture were in decline and a breathing space was needed before the Party could think about building socialism. NEP restored the market economy and money but the commanding heights of the economy (heavy industry, transport, communications, energy) remained state owned.

The Civil War

Civil wars are usually more savage and merciless than wars between states. The Russian Civil War pitted Russian against Russian, Cossack against Cossack, Ukrainian against Ukrainian, not to speak of non-Russians against Russians. Civil war was almost inevitable in Russia given the Bolshevik desire to rule the whole country. They had won in Petrograd but then had

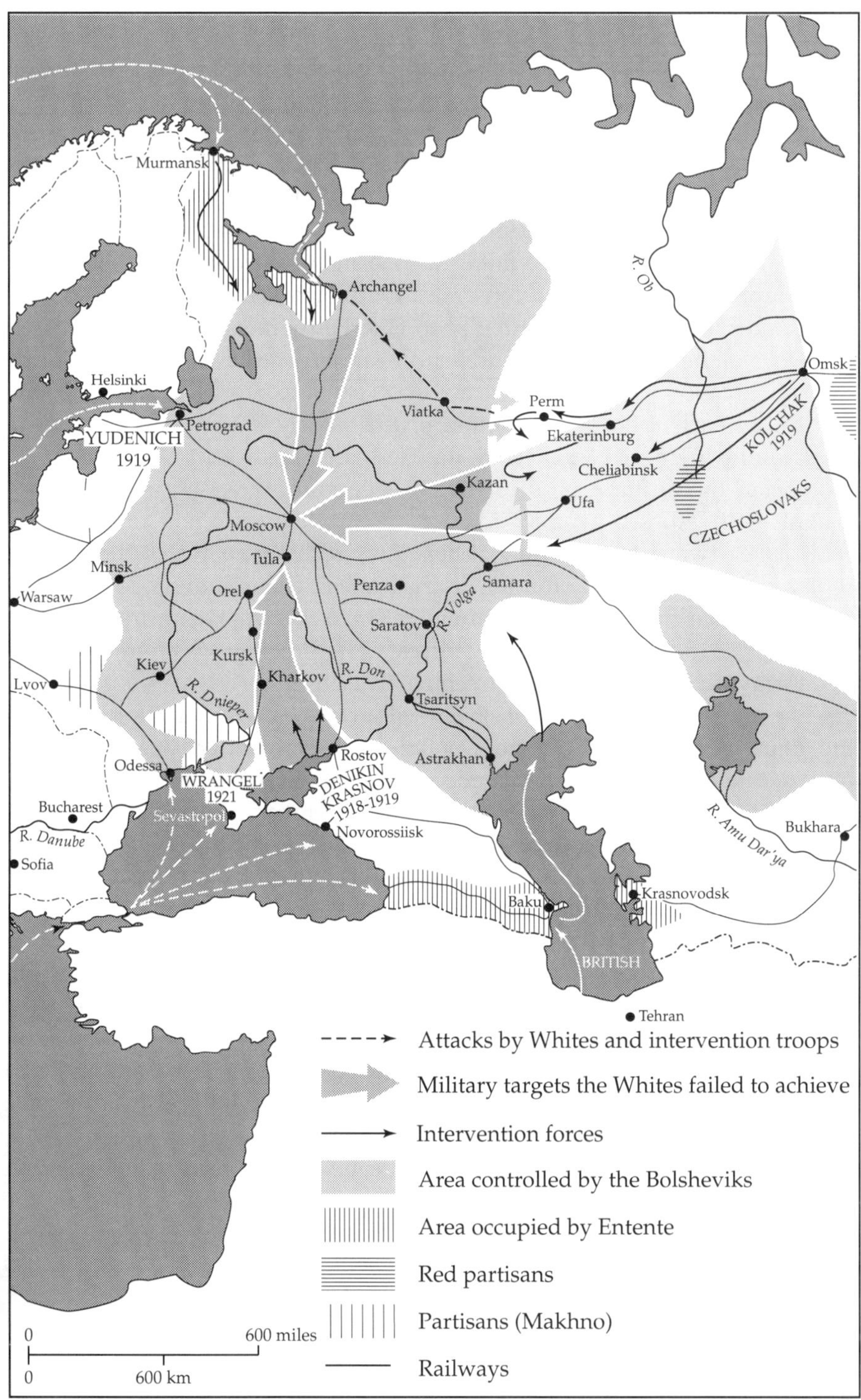

The Civil War, 1919-22: Bolsheviks' defence of the October Revolution

to consolidate their power over the largest country in the world. They wished to dispossess the previous ruling class and property owners. It was unlikely that the latter would hand over everything to the Reds without a fight. There were national communists in Ukraine who believed that Ukraine would be better off independent of Moscow. Lenin could not permit this as Ukraine was economically vital to Russia. Muslims and other nationalities wanted autonomy or independence (see map on page 67). The Allies did not want Russia to fall under German control and intervened.

Fighting was in three main areas, the North West, the South and the East. Kerensky's immediate attempt to take Petrograd failed but it was not until November that Moscow was fully under Bolshevik control. During the war Trotsky, Commander of the Red Army, expanded it from 7,000 to 800,000 by early 1919 and 5 million in 1920. Early Red Army advances in the Ukraine were driven back by the Germans. East of Moscow, for some months in the autumn of 1918, the 40,000-strong Czech Army (who had fought with Russia against Austria) controlled all the Trans-Siberian Railway eastward from Kazan. When the Czech threat was settled it was replaced by Kolchak, a former Tsarist naval commander. He ruled 12 million people from his headquarters in Omsk. Kolchak captured Perm in December 1918 but, thereafter, his forces' only direction was retreat and the Red Army occupied Omsk in November 1919.

In the South, the first anti-Bolshevik army was formed North East of the Black Sea and from there Denikin, its commander, began a three-pronged attack on Moscow. His advance reached Orel, some 400 km south of Moscow, but a decisive defeat there on 20 October 1919 led to his troops' retreat, and, after an unsuccessful stand at Rostov in January 1920, retreat continued to the Black Sea. While Denikin threatened from the South Yudenich began an ambitious attack on Petrograd from the West in October 1919 and nearly succeeded, but he, too, had to retreat and by mid November his troops were disarmed in Estonia. Peasant armies, in particular in the South, were formed to protect the land peasants had seized from 1917. The most noteworthy was the army led by Makhno, an anarchist, and an outstanding general, in Ukraine which both inflicted defeats on Denikin's forces in 1919 and threatened Soviet power in the area in 1920 before final defeat by the Red Army in 1921.

Opponents of Bolshevik power were helped by foreign intervention from Britain, France, USA and Japan but most of the troops had left by the end of 1919. What the foreign armies did provide, however, was equipment for the anti-Bolsheviks. Britain provided Denikin, for example, with 200,000 rifles and 200 guns and Yudenich was also supplied. Further foreign involvement came from Poland. A Polish army, formed after the creation of Poland by the Versailles Peace in 1919, attacked Russian territory in April 1920 with the purpose of detaching some non-Russian territory. Kiev, the Ukrainian capital, was occupied on 6 May. The Poles were then driven back by the Red Army to Warsaw, before the Red Army was forced to retreat until East of Kiev. Anxious to deal with what proved to be the last threat, by Wrangel in the south, peace and negotiations began and were completed by the Treaty of Riga (1921) by which Poland gained more land in western Russia. Wrangel's military operations, June to November 1920, led to retreat and defeat.

On Saturday 6 November 1920, the eve of the third anniversary of the October Revolution, in the Bolshoi Theatre in Moscow, Lenin raised his arms and exclaimed jubilantly: 'Today, we can celebrate our victory'. There was still a minor problem in the Crimea where Wrangel was holding out against the Reds. On 15 November Frunze, the Red commander, reported the taking of Sebastopol, the naval base in the Crimea. The titanic struggle was over. Soviet power was secure and the Bolsheviks were victorious.

Why the Bolsheviks Succeeded in October, Consolidated Their Power and Won the Civil War

- By October, the Bolsheviks had control of the Petrograd Soviet, its Military Revolutionary Committee, and were influential in the army. The Provisional Government was thus shorn of its instruments of coercion (it could also not call on the police to defend it) and, hence, the armed takeover met little resistance.
- No other political party wanted to take power between February and October. The SRs could wait for the Constituent Assembly which would see them as the leading party in the country, the Mensheviks believed that Russia needed to develop into a strong industrial economy before the working class could consider taking power. The Kadets and Octobrists were too small to have mass appeal and wanted the status quo.
- Lenin's leadership was a decisive factor.
- The Bolsheviks had a coherent ideology, a set of goals which were enormously attractive in the confused period of pre-October. They promised the workers power, the peasants, land, the nationalities, national self-determination, an end to exploitation, a bountiful future for everyone, justice for all, and freedom from want.
- After October, there was no organised opposition which had mass appeal. The Mensheviks opposed worker power as a myth and would not use force. The SRs were left without a policy when Lenin took over their policy of land to the peasants. The left SRs wanted to promote world revolution and tried to assassinate Lenin and other leading Bolsheviks. They were the only party which offered armed resistance to the Reds. Their vain revolt in the summer of 1918 allowed the Bolsheviks to suppress them ruthlessly.
- The German threat until March 1918 and the Civil War was an

opportunity for the communists to transform Russia into a fortress under siege and to deploy dictatorial methods which would have been resisted vigorously in peacetime.

- The Bolsheviks always had a clear goal: save the revolution and Soviet power. They could accuse their opponents of being the enemies of Soviet power and socialism. They knew how to mobilise the population for their goals whereas the Whites were quite inept at rallying the ordinary people.
- The Bolsheviks had the skill to develop three institutions which ensured their power: the Communist Party, the Red Army and the Cheka.
- The Red terror which arose in response to White terror in 1918, expanded and proved a fearful weapon against class enemies but also those communists who opposed the centre's policies.
- The Bolsheviks controlled the industrial heartland of the country whereas the Whites were always on the periphery, often dependent on the Allies supplying them with arms and equipment. This led to the Bolsheviks labelling the Whites as traitors to Russia, selling out to western imperialism.
- The Whites (opponents of the new government) underestimated the Reds and thought that time was on their side.
- The Reds (supporters of the government) had a unified command, mainly consisting of ex-Tsarist officers, whereas there were various White commanders and various fronts which made it impossible, given the size of the country, to co-ordinate their attacks.
- The peasants believed the Bolsheviks when they told them that a White victory would mean the return of the landlords.
- The Civil War was a time of great confusion and Bolshevik power almost collapsed several times. Competing soviets were set up everywhere, notably in Ukraine. Here there were soviets which supported independence for Ukraine, Ukraine as part of a loose federation with Russia and anarchist soviets, supporters of Makhno, who wanted to run their own areas without outside interference.
- Trotsky proved an able military leader, learning military affairs as he went along. He was ruthless and pushed through the recruitment of former Tsarist officers as necessary to secure victory. He had Lenin's ear but he fell out time and again with Stalin. This conflict affected the Reds negatively, especially in the Polish campaign.
- The Kronstadt uprising was a watershed for the Bolsheviks. It was the first time that former supporters had turned against them. It was especially embarrassing as the Kronstadt sailors were viewed as the reddest of the red. They wanted democracy and to run their own soviet but Lenin could not allow this. The spilling of so much blood

underlined the utter ruthlessness of the Bolsheviks and their commitment to violence whenever necessary.

- Had the Constituent Assembly remained in session for more than one day in January 1918 it would have challenged the legitimacy of the Bolshevik government. It had an SR majority and would have reflected agrarian socialist values and a government elected by the Assembly would have been a coalition government. Its dispersal (quite illegal) made life easier for the Bolsheviks.

In the Civil War the Reds lost about 125,000 killed in action and over 300,000 who died from disease and wounds. The Whites suffered 175,000 killed in action and over 150,000 died from disease and wounds.

Lenin's Ideology

Now let us attempt a definition of Leninism (note that it goes through two, distinct phases): Phase One. Lenin regarded monopoly capitalism (banks and enterprises which enjoyed a monopoly ran the state in their interests) as a stepping stone to socialism. He wrote in 1916:

> ... the big banks are the state apparatus which we need to bring about socialism, and which we take ready made from capitalism ... A single State Bank, the biggest of the big, with branches in every rural district, in every factory, will constitute as much as nine tenths of the socialist apparatus. This will be country wide bookkeeping, country wide accounting of the production and distribution of goods, this will be ... the skeleton of socialist society ... We can lay hold of and set in motion this state apparatus ... at one stroke, by a single decree, because the actual work of bookkeeping, control, registering, accounting and counting is performed by employees, the majority of whom themselves lead a proletarian or semi-proletarian existence.

Hence, economics takes precedence over politics. The future socialist state will be concerned, first and foremost, with economic growth.

The state, he believed, could not be reformed. Monopoly capitalism and the state were like Siamese twins and in order to smash monopoly capitalism the state had to be smashed as well. The model for Lenin was the Paris Commune of 1871. A commune state could come into being in Russia with the soviets running it. Unlike conventional states it did not need a bureaucracy or a standing army or the divisions of power between the legislature, the executive and the judiciary. Public business was carried out by elected officials accountable to their constituents, liable to be recalled at any time and paid an average workmen's wages. Police functions would be carried out by a militia formed from a universally armed people. Socialism here meant democracy from below. This vision is expressed in the April Theses. One of the reasons for changing the name of the Party into Communist Party was Lenin's obsession with the Paris Commune whose objective had been to dissolve the state into society. This simplistic view of the state - the bearer of everything that was evil and wrong in the world - was to have an immense influence on the future development of Russia. It put out of bounds any discussion about improving its institutions and procedures, making its officials accountable and subjecting its decisions to judicial review. In the Soviet Union there was little discussion about the conduct of elections, access to the media, the immunity of elected representatives, etc. There could not be any discussion of individual and political rights. Lenin regarded the state and politics as having no autonomy or permanence. Both would disappear as exploitation of man by man disappeared. Hence, the goal of Lenin in power was economic rather than political - to eliminate exploitation and thereby eliminate classes. When this had been done there would be no need for the state or politics.

Economic goals would be decided by the Party leadership and not through debate or dispute. The available resources (capital and labour) would be allocated, in a planned and rational manner, in order to achieve an optimal outcome. The allocation of rewards within society would depend on the contribution of individuals and groups to the production achieved by society. Hence, Lenin never suggested that economic priorities be debated by society but would be decided by the Party leadership in consultation with economists, engineers and other specialists. Lenin had nothing but contempt for politics.

Phase Two. In 1920-1 Lenin (together with Trotsky and Bukharin) reformulate the Soviet view of the state. They agreed that socialism could

The end of capitalism. A poster from 1919

no longer be identified with mass popular participation in the management of political, economic and social affairs. Proletarian power was to cease being identified with workers' control, factory committees, trade unions, soviets, people's militias and co-operatives. They agree that the above was merely the first, destructive phase of the revolution because it had produced nothing positive - the country was on the verge of economic ruin. Lenin now concluded that socialism had no longer anything to do with altering the power relations among men but rather transforming their productive relations so that economic growth would eventually lead to abundance and, hence, social freedom. For the first time Bolshevik leaders make a distinction between socialism and communism - hitherto the terms had been used almost interchangeably. Communism is now a long, long way off. The desperate times led to new slogans: iron discipline, ruthless and firm leadership, one man management, and universal labour mobilisation.

The dictatorship of the proletariat is redefined. The dictatorship could not be exercised by the working class as a whole. The dream of a commune state with universal participatory democracy was no longer valid. Only the *avant garde* of the class, endowed with special knowledge and wisdom, was capable of leading the proletariat and running the state. That *avant garde* was to be found in the Party. Communists were a small minority in Russia and this led to the view that allowing competing political views or a free press would result in the Bolsheviks losing power. They had to be suppressed. As Lenin put it succinctly: 'We have no desire to commit suicide'. Lenin then defined what he meant by dictatorship: 'nothing more or less than authority untrammelled by any laws, absolutely unrestricted by any rules whatsoever, and based directly on force. The term dictatorship has no other meaning than this.' Anyone who opposed the Bolsheviks was classified as 'bourgeois' and, hence, could be legitimately destroyed. This included socialists, such as Mensheviks and SRs. Lenin (and Trotsky and Bukharin), in 1920, agreed that the Russian proletariat had become *déclassé* or declassed and had ceased to exist as a proletariat. The result of this sad state of affairs was that the proletarian state would have to use coercion to re-educate the working class. The Kronstadt uprising was a graphic example of this policy in action. The Kronstadters wanted to revert to commune democracy but Lenin wanted his new dictatorship.

Insisting on a monopoly of power, given very limited public support, led to state terror and coercion. Lenin and Bukharin acknowledged that they were behaving in the manner of the imperialist state they wished to destroy throughout the world.

Socialism was redefined in 1920-1 not as mass participation in administering the state but as the most efficient means for allocating capital and labour to maximise output. Democracy was a luxury which could be dispensed with. Lenin was blunt: 'industry is indispensable, democracy is not.' As long as the conflict between capitalism and socialism lasted, Lenin and the Bolsheviks did not promise any 'freedom or any democracy'.

Lenin now summed up politics as nothing more than a concentrated expression of economics.

The essential element of the consolidation of the workers as a class was their consolidation into a single political party. The Communist Party would instil a socialist consciousness and organise the workers nationally, without which they could not exist as a class. The Party would purge the workers of their illusions and educate them through propaganda and practical involvement so that they would eventually come to realise that they had nothing in common with the former economic order in Russia.

As Russia developed economically, Lenin believed politics would recede into the background. Engineers and agronomists would take over. As Lenin put it: 'Henceforth less politics will be the best politics.'

As Lenin lost faith in the creative potential of the proletariat, his faith in science grows. As a method of reasoning it was vastly superior to the disputes of the Party theorists or the untutored mumblings of the masses.

Lenin hated pluralism and always believed that there was one correct view, the working class had only one will to realise its role in history, there was only one path to paradise and only the Party, and the Party alone, knew the way and could guide the proletariat to the Promised Land of freedom and plenty.

At the 2nd Congress of the Comintern, in July 1920, Lenin laid down for the first time the organisational structures of a Communist Party. The core of this organisation is democratic centralism. No individual or lower Party body may dissent from or oppose instructions from a superior body. The penalty for this offence is expulsion. Lenin, at the 10th Party Congress in 1921 fumes: 'we want no more opposition ... we are not a debating society'. A resolution was passed banning factionalism (opposition). The penalty again was expulsion from the Party.

Questions to Consider

- Why did the Tsar lose power in February 1917?
- Did dual power doom the Provisional Government from the very beginning?
- What should the moderate socialists and the government have done to stem the advance of the Bolsheviks?
- What institutions did the Bolsheviks found, to keep themselves in power?
- Why did the Reds win the Civil War? Examine the roles of Lenin, Stalin and Trotsky over the years 1917-21.

EXAMINATION QUESTIONS

1 How much did the triumph of the Bolshevik Party in Russia, between 1917 and 1921, owe to the support of the people?

2 Analyse the reasons which enabled the Bolsheviks to remain in power in Russia and the Soviet Union throughout the years 1919-24.

5 Political Strife: Stalin and His Enemies, 1922-28

In 1921 the civil war on the battlefield was over but the civil war within the Bolshevik leadership was only just beginning. The internal battle was also about power, not between those who wanted Soviet power and those who did not, but between those who wanted to advance rapidly to socialism and those who did not. All communists accepted that socialism was the goal but what did this mean? How, for instance, did one build socialism? The struggle for power (who was boss) went through various phases:

1: Until the Death of Lenin in January 1924

As long as Lenin was sound of mind and limb, he remained the dominant leader, because of his political and intellectual gifts. Stalin, later, would silence his critics: Lenin did not need to do this. He believed he could out argue anyone - providing, of course, he or she was a Bolshevik. Lenin did not waste any breath debating with non-Bolsheviks. Those around Lenin fought among themselves for the ear and praise of the master. This does not mean that they always obeyed Lenin. In fact, Lenin lost several arguments in the Party leadership but never gave up and came back time and again in an attempt to win. Hence, it is not true to say that democracy was stamped out in Soviet Russia by 1921; it did exist within the Party Politburo. Soviet Russia would have developed differently had Lenin not fallen ill in 1922 and died in January 1924. He was a worried man in 1922; he was concerned about the expansion of the bureaucracy, which meant there were more and more officials telling the people what they could, and could not, have and do. He was also concerned about the arrogance of Russian communists in non-Russian areas but, above all, he was worried about the inability of Stalin and Trotsky to get on. He saw this conflict as one which could do great harm to the Party and the country. He even went so far in his Testament to recommend that Stalin be removed from his position as general secretary of the Party. He expected Trotsky to take over from him when he was gone but he accepted that Bukharin was the 'darling of the Party'. Lenin did not think, as a Marxist, that he should name a successor; that was for the Party to decide. Since the others accepted that Trotsky was number two, it concentrated the minds of everyone who did not want Trotsky to become number one.

2: From the Death of Lenin to the Defeat of Trotsky, 1925

The civil war within the Party leadership was between Trotsky, on the one hand, and Stalin, Kamenev, Zinoviev and Bukharin on the other. One can view Trotsky and his allies as being on the left because they were more radical. What were the main issues over which there was conflict?

i) Trotsky was viewed as an internationalist who was willing to put the Soviet revolution at risk in order to promote *world revolution.* This was rather unfair to Trotsky but politics is about labels and perceptions, not about objective reality. In order to counter Trotsky someone had to come up with a Russia first policy. Stalin proved capable of this and his concept is called socialism in one country which he presented to the Russian public in December 1924. His argument boiled down to the assertion that it was possible for socialism to be victorious in one country, obviously Russia, but of course, it could never be secure until the final victory of socialism worldwide.

ii) *The New Economic Policy* was accepted as a temporary retreat from socialism. How long would this transition period last? How was the capital needed for industrialisation to be raised? Socialism would rest on an ever expanding industrial base and this, in turn, would increase the number of workers in the country, who would be natural members of the Communist Party. Trotsky supported the views of the economist Evgeny Preobrazhensky who advocated extracting more taxes from the peasants so as to provide the money to industrialise. Trotsky warned that if the state did not give greater priority to the industrial sector Soviet Russia was running the risk of being dominated by rich peasants (kulaks) and NEP traders. This sent a shiver down many communist spines. Bukharin responded for the right wing which supported NEP. Their view was that attempting to squeeze the peasant would lead to disaster. Peasants would stop producing for the market and concentrate on feeding themselves and their families. Why should a peasant work harder so as to pay higher taxes? Bukharin came out with the slogan: 'Peasants, enrich yourselves!' He saw agricultural growth as the way ahead for Soviet Russia. The greater the output the greater the tax revenue, and the greater the demand by the rural sector for industrial goods. This, in turn, would stimulate industrial expansion.

There were two opposing views on economic growth, the organic or genetic and the teleological. The first, held by Bukharin and the right, was that an economy should develop naturally. Since Russia was a predominantly agrarian economy, agriculture would lead growth. The other school, the teleologists, advocated setting a goal for the future and then devoting all the resources of the state to achieve it. It will occur to the reader that Stalin supported the organic school at this time but, in 1928, went over to the teleological school.

iii) The Bolshevik leaders were greatly taken by the lessons of the French Revolution, one of which was that the revolution could be hijacked by a general. This caused them to fear that Trotsky, the maker of the Red Army and the Commissar for War might use his position to stage a coup. Trotsky, in fact, never harboured his desire and suspicion of him was unfounded. Nevertheless, Trotsky was manoeuvred into giving up his position as Commissar for War in 1925 and, thereby, abandoned his last great state office.

3: 1925 to the Defeat of the Left Opposition, December 1927

i) Kamenev and Zinoviev, alarmed at the increase in power of Stalin after Trotsky's resignation as Commissar for War, changed sides. Now they joined forces with Trotsky against Stalin and Bukharin. However, they found it difficult to co-ordinate their efforts with Trotsky but, in 1926-7, they managed to forge the United Opposition to Stalin. This group attracted many of the great names of the revolution but their greatest weakness was their lack of institutional bases from which to attack Stalin and the right. Zinoviev was removed as Party leader in January 1926 and Kamenev was removed as deputy chair of Sovnarkom a month later.

ii) Trotsky and his supporters were defeated at a CC plenum in April 1926 and the United Opposition attempted to present their case for accelerated industrialisation and more democracy in the Party at the 15th Party Conference in October 1926 but were denied the right to speak. Frustrated, they took to addressing workers in factories and in the open air but their meetings were broken up by militants and they were investigated by the GPU. This was the first time that Party members had used violence against other Party members. Now the opposition had to function in secret. When they attempted to prepare a statement to be presented to delegates at the 15th Party Congress, December 1927, their printing press was discovered by the GPU and their activity was labelled criminal. It is ironical that Trotsky had supported the ban on factionalism (opposing the policies of the leadership) within the Party at the 10th Party Congress, March 1921. Now that resolution was used by Stalin to demand and get the expulsion of Trotsky, Kamenev, Zinoviev and others from the Party. This marked the end of the United Opposition.

4: December 1927 to the Defeat of Bukharin and the Right, 1929

i) Stalin was very astute after the Congress and offered to readmit members of the United Opposition to the Party if they recanted and promised to follow Party policy. This split the opposition, with Kamenev and Zinoviev performing the ritual of *mea culpa* (my fault) and denouncing Trotsky and Trotskyism. Trotsky and his closest associates were made of sterner stuff

and refused to bow the knee. They were dispatched to Alma Ata and later packed off abroad.

ii) Bukharin was alarmed by the victory of Stalin and the shape the Party was taking. He contacted Kamenev to see what they could do to halt the inevitable rise of Stalin. He, by now, had taken over the economic views of the left and the draft first Five Year Plan was presented to the Party in 1928. It involved collectivisation of the peasantry and rapid industrialisation. Those who had doubts of such a breakneck rush for economic growth and the wisdom of exploiting the peasants were grouped together by Stalin as the Right Opposition. The key members were Bukharin, Rykov, chair of Sovnarkom, and Tomsky, head of the trade unions. The did not stand much of a chance against Stalin as he now had many allies in the Party organisations, trade unions and other institutions and could set them on the Right Opposition. By this time it was virtually impossible to publish anything in the Party press which did not support the official line. By late 1929 the Right had succumbed and performed the usual ritual of admitting their mistakes, asking for forgiveness, and asking to be allowed to stay in public life.

Reasons for Stalin's Success Against His Rivals

How did Stalin build up his position and why was he successful in outmanoeuvring the other leading Bolsheviks?

- Stalin had luck on his side. Had Lenin not died Stalin would probably have been sent to the provinces to work for the Party. Dzerzhinsky, the head of the Cheka, from its inception to his death in 1926 was never one of Stalin's fans. His death allowed Stalin to infiltrate his supporters into the political police and eventually use them against his opponents.
- Stalin possessed the organisational skill to develop the Party secretariat into a major power base. When appointed general secretary in 1922 the position was regarded as nothing more than that of a glorified clerk. Stalin was also a member of the Politburo, as well as the Organisational Bureau (responsible for cadres and other matters) and had other posts, such as Commissar for Nationalities (October 1917-July 1923) and head of the Workers' and Peasants' Inspectorate (supervising state officials) (February 1920-April 1922). He listened in to the private Kremlin telephone network and thus was well informed about what his colleagues thought.
- Stalin was based in Moscow from 1921 onwards and thus was privy to everything that was going on. Many of his colleagues had duties which took them away from the capital and consumed their energies. Zinoviev, for example, was Party leader in Leningrad, Kamenev was deputy Prime Minister.
- Stalin always liked to play the role of mediator in the early phase of the

revolution. He would listen to their arguments and then propose a compromise solution. In this way he came to be seen as a moderate. Stalin had an elephantine memory and stored all the information away, for future use.

- Stalin had the ability to recruit persons who wanted a career and preferred working in the Party apparatus to working in a factory. In the early years Stalin could not openly brief them on what to do (loyally to support him) but they got the message all the same.
- Stalin's control over personnel affairs in the Party secretariat permitted him to sack those who sided with the opposition. Every time a leading politician lost, this would be followed by a purge of his supporters.
- Greater influence over local Party affairs resulted in delegates who supported Stalin's line being elected to Party Congresses and the Central Committee.
- Lenin, at the 10th Party Congress (1921), had forced through the ban on factionalism. It was also agreed that if two-thirds of the CC agreed, a comrade could be expelled from the CC, and eventually the Party. Stalin was able to use this and claim that he was carrying out Lenin's will. If he secured a two-thirds majority in the CC, he could reform the Party according to his own objectives. Control of the media also meant that opponents could not publish within the law.
- There was no tradition of party politics in Russia so politicians were not used to the give and take and compromise of democratic politics. Russian politics became a matter of eliminating the other political parties and policies.
- The low level of culture in Russia, especially among Bolshevik supporters, made it easier to misrepresent opponents' points of view. Stalin grasped very quickly that communists were looking for a simplified version of Marxism which they could comprehend. Stalin provided this in his writings which were presented in very direct, simple language.
- Stalin presented himself as the leading disciple of Lenin and in this way was able to present his analysis of Lenin's thought to the masses. He could select passages from Lenin which supported his position. Trotsky, on the other hand, ridiculed this attempt to 'dissect' Lenin but failed to grasp the political significance of so doing.
- Stalin, although a Georgian by nationality, understood the advantage of promoting Russian nationalism. The concept of socialism in one country pandered to the Russian need to feel important in the world and to force other nations to respect them.
- Stalin never took on all his opponents at the same time: he preferred to challenge them one by one or in small groups. Hence, the first opponent was Trotsky, then Trotsky, Kamenev and Zinoviev (but when

Document: Here is Stalin's definition of the Party in 1924

1. The Party is the vanguard of the working class ...
2. The Party is the organised detachment of the working class ...
3. The Party is the highest form of class organisation of the proletariat ...
4. The Party is the instrument of the dictatorship of the proletariat ...
5. The Party is the embodiment of the unity of will, incompatible with the existence of factions ...
6. The Party is strengthened by purging itself of opportunist elements ...

Trotsky had already been weakened), then Bukharin. The other side of this coin was his ability to forge coalitions against his opponents. These coalitions only lasted until the opponent was defeated, then he would set about constructing another coalition. It was usual for his coalition partners to lead the assault on his opponents, with Stalin in the background. He only became high profile when he believed that he had finally won.

- Stalin was never totally committed to any policy: he was like a butterfly flitting from one approach to socialism to the other. He was on the right against Trotsky and the left against Bukharin. This reveals that he was playing a tactical game. Trotsky did not believe that he had any socialist convictions but this was wrong - Stalin was always on the left but could not reveal this while Trotsky was around.
- Stalin was very skilled in spotting the weaknesses of his opponents and in devising tactics to outmanoeuvre them. This meant that he needed to know how someone would react so as to plan the next move, ahead of time.
- Stalin was aware that the successful mobilisation of the state during the Civil War provided many lessons for the future. The first Five Year Plan, which launched industrialisation and the collectivisation of agriculture, was the great challenge. Everyone and everything were to be mobilised in order to make the country great. The stronger the country, the more secure Stalin was.

Stalin's rise to power was not inevitable but the Party and state Lenin built permitted him to make the most of his organisational talents. Also, there was no dangerous external threat to Soviet Russia in the 1920s, that was to come in the 1930s. Had Hitler come to power in Germany in the early 1920s, the world might now look very different as the Red Army could not have defeated the German army in the 1920s and 1930s.

The Purges, 1936-8

In 1936 a remarkable series of events, the purges, began and continued until abruptly ended in 1938. Initiated by Stalin, probably to replace the old guard élites in the Party, the government and the NKVD, as well as management élites and, particularly, the non-Russian élites in the republics (see Russification, pages 96-7), the purges took on a momentum of their own and at local level seem to have been out of control. The only groups who escaped were workers, non-Kulak peasants and, in general, academic scientists: any truth in the allegations in the trials became less and less important. As the purges developed at the local level they followed no consistent pattern but Stalin realised they could serve his purpose to create a new *nomenklatura* and a terrified obedience by the people (see, also, page 90).

The number of people purged is unknown, probably between 7 and 14 million. Some were shot but most were sent to labour camps, the *gulags*, where many died from exhaustion and disease. Firm conclusions about the purges are difficult until there is access to more information. The revisionist view is that, once started, they developed a life of their own at local level to relieve the hardship and suffering endured during the Five Year Plans. The idealism of the first Five Year Plan was replaced, after 1932, by disillusion because hard work was not rewarded with higher living standards: during the purges Party and government officials paid the price.

The consequences of the purges included increased effort by managers and officials, so as to avoid the same fate themselves, and an increase in Stalin's power. In retrospect, this was especially helpful in the army in which, despite the military reverses of 1941-2 after Germany's invasion, Stalin's leadership was unquestioned.

Questions to Consider

- What are the keys to Stalin's success in his conflict with his rivals?
- Given the desire of communists to speed up industrialisation after 1921, why was Trotsky so unsuccessful?
- Explain how Stalin built up coalitions against his rivals. Why did they not realise that he was playing them off against each other so that they would all lose and he would win?
- 'The main reason behind forced collectivisation was political, not economic.' Discuss.
- What sections of society benefited most from the 1930s? Which lost most?
- Stalin told lies all the time. Why did he get away with it?

EXAMINATION QUESTIONS

1 How did Stalin gain and consolidate his power?
2 Were Stalin's purges 'necessary to save the revolution' in Russia?
3 To what extent was Stalin's desire for complete political control the prime motivation behind the purges and why was there so little resistance to them?
4 Why did the rulers of the Soviet Union bring about the deaths of millions of their subjects in the 1930s?

6 Economic and Social Change, 1928-41

The Five Year Plans

The Five Year Plans were the greatest experiment in rapid economic growth ever seen anywhere in the world. They were attended by extraordinary optimism and this added vitality to the efforts of those who believed sincerely they were building a better world. It was a colossal gamble and Stalin admitted as much to Churchill during the war against Germany. It achieved more than sound economic advice would ever have advocated. It transformed the Soviet Union from being an also ran in the industrial stakes into one of the lead runners. It was possible because the Soviet Union had abundant resources of raw materials and labour. They had everything except rubber. No other country on Earth is as blessed as the USSR. Hence, what the Russians achieved could not have been achieved in any other country except the United States. The soviets were able to industrialise on their own. The imported technology during the first Five Year Plan but cut back during the second. This method of economic expansion was only possible during an era of relatively simple technology. It would now be totally impracticable. Soviet industrialisation was based on the metal industries, energy and construction. It had two purposes, to build up a powerful industrial base and to provide a defence economy which would produce the sinews of war. An example of this was that every pilot and aircraft had a dual function: they were for peacetime but also wartime use. The rapidly expanding economies of today in the Pacific Rim have adopted a totally different industrialisation strategy. They base their growth on exports and thereby acquire the capital to import advanced technology. They are always trying to improve their products because if they do not do so their competitors will take over their markets. They all wish to compete successfully in the world market economy. This also applies to the People's Republic of China.

The mentality in Soviet Russia in the 1930s was totally different. The Russians deliberately set out to eliminate the market economy in their country. They disregarded cost and made quantitative targets their goal. They could do this since they did not need to export to survive. They had opted out of competing in world markets. This had great advantages but even greater disadvantages. It allowed Soviet industry to expand at a time when the rest of the world was in recession and export markets were difficult. They were not dependent on imports to grow. They imported little capital and decided to generate it themselves. However they paid a heavy price for their industrial experiment. Lack of attention to costs led to colossal waste and the mentality that there was no need to husband raw materials. The quantitative approach inevitably meant a decline in quality. Quality control was neglected in the rush to meet planned targets. The emphasis on heavy industry led to an imbalance in the economy. Everything connected with heavy industry and defence got priority, everything else was sacrificed in their name. The high rate of investment was achieved by cutting living standards and exploiting the labour force. The forced collectivisation of agriculture, considered necessary to ensure a guaranteed supply of food to the new cities and building sites, damaged Soviet agriculture and, under communism, it never recovered. Life was so miserable in the countryside that the ambitious and intelligent left.

The Soviet Economy During the 1930s

Table 6.1: Fulfilment of principal goals of the first and second Five Year Plans. Figures are per cent. (Jasny was a Russian-American economist.)

	First FYP (1928-32)	*Second FYP (1933-7)*
National Income (official Soviet)	91.5	96.1
Jasny estimate	70.2	66.5
Industrial Production		
Official Soviet	100.7	103.0
Jasny estimate	69.9	81.2
Agricultural Production		
Official Soviet	57.8	68.8
Jasny estimate	49.6	76.7
Employment		
Workers and employees	144.9	93.4
Industry, workers and employees	173.9	-
Wages (workers and employees)		
Average monthly wage	143.9	173.6
Average real wage, official Soviet	31.9	102.6
Average real wage, Zalesky estimate	26.0	65.8
Labour Productivity, Industry		
Official Soviet	65.1	-
Jasny estimate	41.8	-
Cost of Production		
Industry	146.1	121.1
Investment		
In constant prices (inflation deducted)	54	-

Stalin, the madman, exploits the people (from Satyricon, *an anti-Bolshevik Russian publication, Paris, 1931)*

Table 6.2: Structural change in the Soviet economy in the 1930s. (Estimates by an American economist.)

	1928	*1937*
Sector Share (%)		
Agriculture	49	31
Industry	28	45
Services	23	24
End use of National Output (%)		
Consumption	82	55
Government	8	22
Net domestic investment	10	23
Foreign Trade		
Exports and imports as a per cent of national output	6.2	1.0
Economic Growth (annual average, %)		
National output: 1928-40	5.1	
Per capita product: 1928-40	3.6	
Per capita product: 1917-41	2.5	

The Development of Agriculture During the 1930s

Table 6.3: Soviet grain production and procurement (million tonnes), 1929-38. (These calculations are by American economists.)

Year	*Grain Production*	*Grain Procurement*	*%*
1929	66.8	10.8	16.2
1930	71.0	16.0	22.5
1931	65.0	22.1	34.0
1932	65.0	23.7	36.5
1933	71.0	23.3	32.8
1934	77.5	28.4	36.6
1935	63.0	25.7	40.8
1936	63.0	25.7	40.8
1937	97.5	31.8	32.6
1938	73.0	31.5	43.1

Official Soviet figures always inflate performance and this was normal for the Stalin and post-Stalin period. Table 6.1 permits a comparison between the official Soviet and a western estimate. (After the collapse of communism in 1991 it transpired that Jasny had been too optimistic about Soviet performance; at the time he was accused of understating performance.) The figures for employment during the first Five Year Plan reveal that many more peasants rushed into industry than planned for. This was reflected in the monthly wages which were way above those calculated for.

However, the only way this could be done was by printing money and increasing inflation. The official Soviet estimate (inflation deducted) is as low as 31.9 per cent of the planned level with Jasny coming in lower. This is an indicator of how low living standards among workers were. They were even lower in the countryside. Due to the expansion of the labour force, labour productivity did not come anywhere near the official target. Costs of production, as a consequence, were much higher than expected.

Table 6.2 shows how rapidly the structure of the Soviet economy changed between 1928 and 1937. Very striking is the huge drop in consumption by the population and the rapid rise of investment, achieved by cutting back living standards. Foreign trade had become almost irrelevant by 1937. The estimate of annual economic growth, 1928-40, puts the whole experiment into perspective. Given the huge sacrifices, 5.1 per cent annual growth is modest and arguably could have been achieved by adopting more traditional methods.

Table 6.3 shows how little progress was made to increase rapidly grain production under collectivisation. There was one remarkable year, 1937, but the next year was back to the average performance of the 1930s. The high state procurement (state purchases at nominal prices) meant that the countryside was often short of food. The failure of collectivisation to meet its plan targets (agriculture never met its targets in any Five Year Plan right up to the end of communism) meant that the country was always short of food.

Specialists of all Hues

When the Bolsheviks took over in 1917 there were not many graduates who supported them. The mayhem of the immediate post-revolution years led many to emigrate and the Cheka killed off some others. The educated were shown little respect. One professor complained to Lenin that a local petty official had ordered him to sleep in the same bed as his (the professor's) wife. The Party could not boast of many members who were engineers. In 1928 a survey revealed that there were only 138 engineers in the Party. Not a very promising augury for the success of the Five Year Plan. Industrial managers were quite different. About three-quarters of them were communists but lacked higher technical qualifications. The Bolsheviks had attempted to give preference to their own supporters during the 1920s in order to train more technical specialists but with limited success since most of them had little basic education. Most engineers thought the goals of the first Five Year Plan unrealistic and were critical of the lowering of standards. The Party decided to show the engineers who was master in the state. A series of sensational trials between 1928 and 1931 aimed at cowing any resistance to economic plans and directives. The Shakhty trial in May 1928 involved Donbass engineers accused of wrecking equipment and organising accidents (the real reason for this state of affairs was the unskilled labour). Stalin warned ominously: 'Wrecking by the bourgeois intelligentsia is one of the most dangerous forms of opposition to developing socialism'. Menshevik economists in Gosplan were accused of the crime of proposing lower growth targets. Food specialists were accused of sabotaging food supplies. This neatly explained why there were always food shortages.

In the educational world the years 1928-31 were a terrible experience for professors and teachers of bourgeois origin. It was a period when students dominated and more attention was paid to practical learning than theoretical. However, a whole new cohort entered higher education,

Aleksandra Kollontai (see page 88). She is the supporter of the fleet, an ambassador and author of the book Love and the Bees

propelled there by the Party in its desire to train specialists loyal to it. Something like a third of students in further education were from the factory floor and Party activists in 1932. The failure rate among them could be as high as 70 per cent and this led to a rethink. Stalin changed his mind about bourgeois specialists in June 1931 and called for them to be shown respect and recruited. The period when the worker could be insolent to a specialist was over. The same applied in education. Back came discipline and out went quotas favouring the working class. It was the intelligentsia which benefited most from the ending of quotas and the sons and daughters of graduates and white collar employees rushed into the technical colleges and universities. They joined the Party as well. By 1937 there were 47,000 communist engineers. Many of them were recruited by the administration and the political police so that one about one-third worked directly in production.

Women and Revolution

Red women were active during the October Revolution and the Civil War (over 70,000 joined up and about 1,800 were killed) and there were many in the Cheka. However, during the 1920s, women become less visible politically and under Stalin there are no women among the top political leaders. Stalinism is profoundly masculine. Aleksandra Kollontai was an influential feminist (she ended up as Soviet ambassador to Sweden) and she espoused all the ideas of pre-war Europe about the future role of women. One of them was that women should be got out of the kitchen. Lenin was against individual flats having kitchens and so the communal kitchen, to be used by several families, became the norm. The revolution proclaimed equality for the sexes and there was a vast amount of legislation stating this. Putting this into practice proved much more difficult. Most men objected to their women being politicised and preferred them to be at home when they came back for their supper instead of being at meetings. The revolution was physically very demanding. Did it leave any time over for sex? Most revolutionaries argued that the revolution was too important for time to be spent on love and sex. To be a revolutionary woman, however, was to be wild. Those who resisted were called bourgeois. Mixed dormitories were usual. This resulted, as one journalist put it, in liberty, equality and maternity - equality for the sexes, liberty for the men and maternity for the women. Free love was a myth, women paid. Lenin thought youth's obsession with sex the modern disease. If Lenin was a conservative, Aran Zalkind was an arch-conservative. He drew up 12 commandments which owed little to the Old Testament. Purely physical sexual desire was impermissible from the revolutionary-proletarian point of view. Sexual attraction to the class enemy was as depraved as a crocodile trying to mate with an orangutan. Sex outside marriage was impermissible and was for reproduction. Couples should cut down on sex and use the stored up energy to further the goals of the revolution.

The Party had its own organisation, the Zhenotdel, but it never had much clout. Women officials copied their male colleagues. Leather jacketed, leather booted, women comrades went around the factories and villages propounding the values and goals of socialism. The family was seen as a bourgeois institution which oppressed women. Couples who cohabited were then recognised as families. Divorce was easy - all that was required was to inform the partner. This could be done by sending a postcard. Not surprisingly the orphan population grew almost out of control. Sex was always on the agenda. There were earnest discussions about sex and revolution. Collectivisation caused great hostility and rumours circulated in one Ukrainian village that the young women were going to be handed over to the men and the old women boiled down to make soap. Abortion was made easy in 1920 but abortion on demand ended in 1936 and it also became more difficult to divorce the same year. Stalin wanted more children to be born and into a stable family. Russian society was reverting to its traditional values.

Society

Stalin had a vision of the new Soviet man and woman, working selflessly for the building of socialism and being model communists - following the advice of the leader without demur. This vision was utopian, the model Soviet person never came into being. However, it could serve as a goal, towards which everyone could be encouraged to strive. Thinking about workers was utopian in the early years of the first Five Year Plan when it was thought that they would sacrifice themselves for the good of the cause. When it was clear that they expected something in return, the state became coercive, imposing strict labour discipline. Part of Stalin's political skill lay in recognising that people needed incentives to work harder, that the state could benefit by setting one person against another and that society was profoundly conservative. Most people wanted what their parents' generation had not had. The traditional family, for instance. There was an attempt to change the seven day week and make it ten days or more. That way you had to work more days before the weekend. This did not catch on.

Three groups emerge in the 1930s as the ruling group which will develop into the ruling class: the technical administrators (engineers and managers), the government and Party. They formed the nucleus of the nomenklatura, the bosses. Movement between these groups was common, engineers became first Party secretaries in many areas because their main task was to supervise industry. Also, they were all Party men - there were few women among these élites. In the military, former political commissars who had proven themselves moved into military academies and when they left took up command posts. The same pattern is discernible in law, health,

education, the diplomatic service and culture. Here Party activists without formal education acquired it and joined the upwardly mobile.

Stalin was aware that the upwardly mobile, once they had acquired their desired position, would become conservative and resistant to change. The tactic adopted to promote change was the permanent purge. The striking factor about the new ruling group was their individual and collective insecurity. The purges of the 1930s affected almost everyone and resulted in millions of deaths. Many of the purges were not lethal. One official would denounce another, when he was sacked the other could take his place. Ordinary citizens could denounce officials and in this way give vent to their frustrations. The murder of Kirov in December 1934 seems to have been the opportunity Stalin was waiting for and indeed he may have been closely implicated in the murder. Before then there had been trials of specialists and opposition politicians but in relatively small numbers. In 1935 all members of the left opposition still at liberty were arrested and attempts made to get them to sign a statement that they were part of a vast conspiracy, run from abroad by Trotsky. The three great Show Trials were theatre where everyone involved had a role to play. The defendants normally confessed to the most outlandish crimes, often after beatings and loss of sleep or promises that they would be spared. If a person was convicted he was an enemy of the people. As such his family was also guilty by association and they could become lepers in society. When a husband was sentenced wives were advised to divorce them. Sentenced officials lost all their privileges, as did their families. The worst year was 1937. Accusations of being a traitor, German or Japanese spy, a member of the Rightist-Trotskyist gang were common and officials disappeared in droves. Some of them were immediately executed, others perished in the labour camps. The period 1936-8 was a collective nightmare for the Soviet population. No one could be certain, except Stalin himself, that there would not be a knock on the door at midnight, resulting in one being dragged out of bed and marched off, often never to return. Was it all orchestrated from the centre by Stalin? This is too simplistic. He gave the signal and his cohorts throughout the country swung into action, determined to overfulfil the plan. Thus the purges developed a momentum of their own. The country was too vast for anyone at the centre to control events. It is important to remember that the majority of officials believed they were helping Stalin and the Party and what they were doing was therefore right.

This made practically everyone two-faced. Officially one agreed with Stalin that life had become better and more cheerful. One stated that the 1936 Soviet constitution was the most democratic in the world but woe betide those who tried to make use of its provisions. One agreed with the verdict of the courts that there were saboteurs, spies, enemies of the people everywhere. This was the public persona. In private, one returned to the real world, faced with the harsh realities and struggle for existence.

Document. The Idolisation of Stalin

This is an extract from a speech by a writer in February 1935. It underlines the semi-divine nature of Stalin and is an example of his personality cult which began in earnest on his 50th birthday in December 1929:

> Thank you, Stalin. Thank you because I am joyful. Thank you because I am well ... Every time I have found myself in his presence I have been subjugated by his strength, his charm, his grandeur. I have experienced a great desire to sing, to cry out, to shout with joy and happiness ... I love a young woman with renewed love and shall perpetuate myself in my children - all thanks to thee, great educator, Stalin ... And when the woman I love presents me with a child the first word it shall utter will be: Stalin.
>
> O great Stalin, O leader of the peoples, Thou who broughtest man to birth, Thou who fructifies the earth, Thou who restorest the centuries ...

However, one had to find the right person to confide in. If one misjudged, one was denounced and that could mean the end. Wives denounced husbands for confessions during moments of intimacy. Perhaps half the population was informing on the other half. It was also a crime not to report incriminating evidence. Everyone became wary of everyone else. Fear walked the streets. The only ones who had little to fear were those on the margin of society. The little man and little woman was much less likely to become a victim.

By 1940 society had returned to its traditional mould. The family was the centre of society, education was for those who passed the entrance examinations - positive discrimination for workers and peasants was a thing of the past - and fees had to be paid for higher education. A ruling group had consolidated its position but was insecure. This new group adopted the tastes of the pre-1917 ruling class, complete with chintz curtains, polka-dotted teacups at home and thick carpets and heavy dark furniture at work. Society was very hierarchical and those above one had to be shown respect and deference. Those below could be bawled at. The socialist world had become conservative, experimentation was over.

Questions to Consider

- 'The main reason behind forced collectivisation was political, not economic.' Discuss.
- What sections of society benefited most from the 1930s? Which lost most?
- Stalin told lies all the time. Why did he get away with it?
- Were the sacrifices the Soviet population made during the 1930s worth while?
- Why was there so much enthusiasm during the first Five Year Plan and why did it then wane?

EXAMINATION QUESTIONS

1 In what ways, and to what extent, can Stalin's policies of collectivisation and industrialisation between 1928-41 be seen as a betrayal of socialist ideals?

2 Why was the New Economic Policy introduced and then abandoned in the Soviet Union?

7 The Non-Russians and Foreign Policy, 1917-41

Poland and Russia are redrawing their frontiers. The new frontier goes right through a Polish peasant's land. The surveyors say to him: 'We can move the frontier a little to put you wholly in Poland or Russia. Which would you prefer? The peasant thinks. 'Poland.' Why? 'Oh! I can't stand the Russian winters!'

Nationality Policy: Lenin

In April 1917 Lenin reformulated Bolshevik nationality policy. In order to win support in non-Russian areas Lenin recognised the federal principle of government and that concessions would be made to the non-Russians. He also suggested that the Communist Party be decentralised and divided along national lines with the setting up of national communist parties. The confirmation that the future Russian state would be a federation was a major concession to the non-Russian nationalities. He recognised that the Communist Party could only secure a monopoly of power in non-Russian areas by combining local nationalism with the political institutions of federalism.

Nationality Policy: Stalin

The first version of Soviet federalism was presented by Stalin in 1920, when People's Commissar for Nationalities, based on the concept of national-territorial autonomy, according to which the whole country would be divided into administrative regions based on nationality composition. Stalin then defined what constituted a nation: 'A nation is an historically constituted stable community of people, formed on the basis of the common possession of four principal criteria: a common language, a common territory, a common economic life, and a common psychological make-up'. How much power should be devolved to these national territories and what powers should Moscow retain for itself? Stalin came up with three types of autonomy: a narrow administrative autonomy (for peoples which had no recognised territory of their own), wider political autonomy (for peoples with some history of administrative unity such as the Volga Germans but they were not to be permitted the right to conduct their own economic or foreign policy or foreign trade) and contractual autonomy (for those who met all four conditions for a nation. These were

Document: Stalin's definition of a nation

A nation is an historically constituted stable community of people, formed on the basis of the common possession of four principal criteria: a common language, a common territory, a common economic life, and a common psychological make-up.

Anthony Smith, a British scholar, suggests the following definitions:

Ethnic Community: a named human population with a myth of common ancestry, shared memories and cultural elements, a link with an historic territory or homeland and a measure of solidarity;

Ethnic category: a group characterised as culturally distinct by outsiders, but possessing little or no sense of common ethnicity;

Nation: a named human population sharing an historic territory, common myths and memories, a mass, public culture, a single territorial economy, and common rights and duties for all members;

Nation State: a nation which is territorial coextensive with a single state and exercises sole power in that state; and

Nationalism: an ideological movement for attaining and maintaining identity, unity and autonomy on behalf of a human population, some of whose members believe it to constitute an actual or potential nation.

Ukraine, Belorussia, Georgia, Armenia and Azerbaijan). Contractual autonomy permitted governments to determine their own domestic and international policies - relations with one another.

The Communists Change Course

The Bolsheviks changed their position in 1921 and redefined contractual autonomy. Moscow had seen the rise of nationalism in the non-Russian republics. Also Russia was facing economic collapse and badly needed access to the raw materials, food and foreign currency in the other republics. Trade was hindered by customs' barriers, different currencies and no unified transport system. At the 10th Party Congress in 1921 Stalin argued that the existence of the national republics undermined their ability to defend themselves against the 'imperialist threat'. He stated that the defence of the achievements of socialism and the recovery of the war-shattered Russian economy required a rethink about the relations of Moscow and the other areas. Stalin's solution was to place all national territories within the Russian Soviet Federal Socialist Republic (RSFSR) as autonomous areas. The regions quickly pointed out that this meant returning to the practice of the Tsarist Empire, with Moscow dominating. In April 1922 Stalin presented a draft federal treaty between the RSFSR and the independent socialist republics. Contractual autonomy disappeared and they were to be incorporated in the RSFSR as autonomous units. The republican communist parties were in favour of union with Russia but not Stalin's system of federalism. Lenin intervened in September 1922 and called the draft an example of Great Russian chauvinism (lording it over other nations). Hence, when the Union of Soviet Socialist Republics came

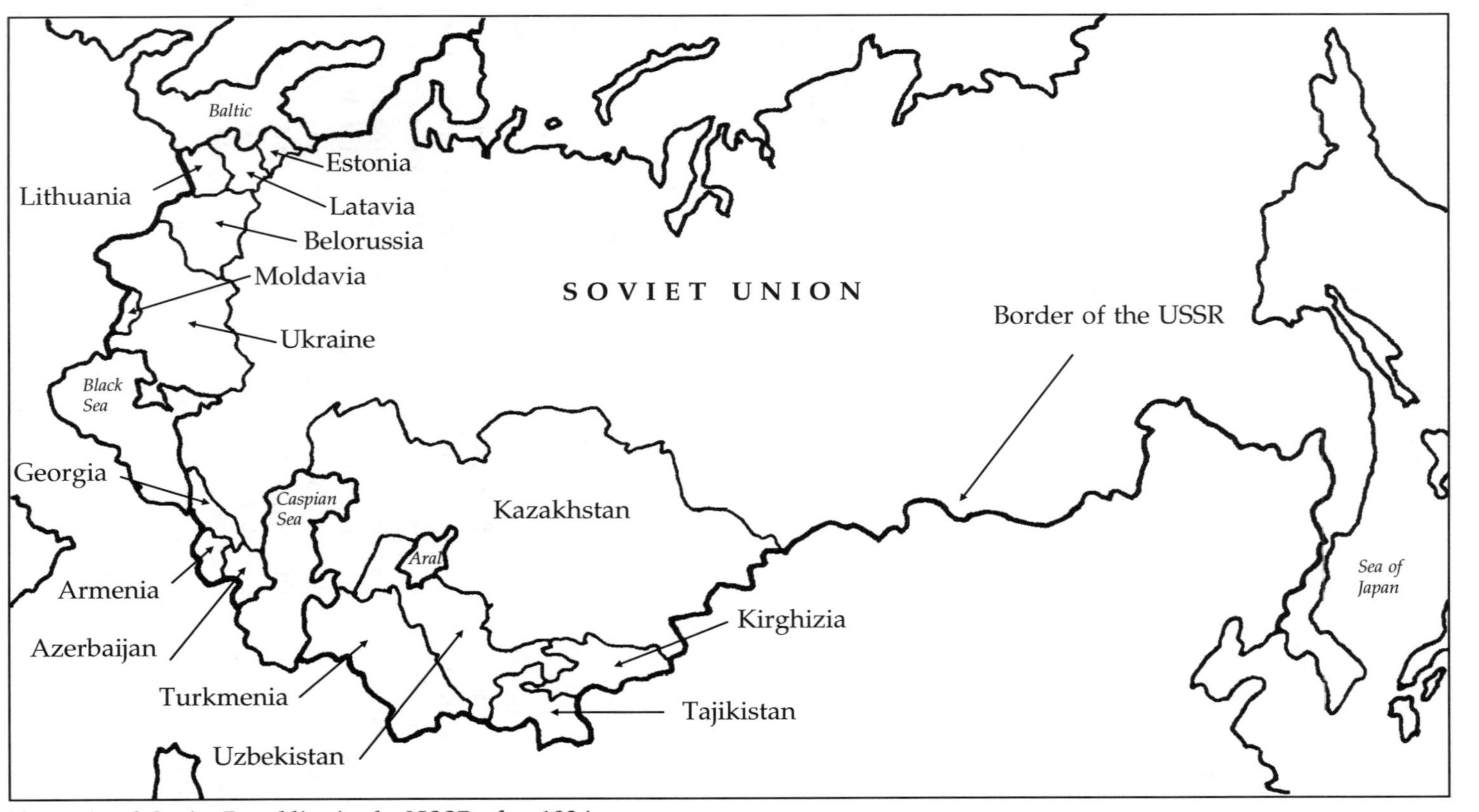

The national Soviet Republics in the USSR after 1924

into being in December 1922 it consisted of four equal republics (the RSFSR, Ukraine, Belorussia and the Transcaucasian Soviet Socialist Republic (comprising Georgia, Armenia and Azerbaijan). The federal treaty divided all peoples into four categories: those which possessed all four criteria of Stalin's definition were nations and became a Union Republic (100,000 people or more) or an Autonomous Republic (less than 100,000). Those peoples who had less than the four criteria were classified as nationalities (*narodnosti*) and were divided into autonomous regions (*oblasts*) and autonomous territories (*okrugs*).

Korenizatsiya

A fundamentally new approach to nationality affairs was adopted at the 13th Party Congress in April 1923. This policy is known as *korenizatsiya* (literally taking root) and envisaged the 'blossoming' of Soviet nationalities which promoted the development of the cultural traditions of the indigenous peoples and the strengthening of their national identities. The first reason for this radical change of course was the lack of Party members in the Union and Autonomous Republics. There were just not enough communists to implement Moscow's policies and a multi-lingual (Russian was the key) and multi-national administrative élite just did not exist. The goal was the creation of Soviet élites in non-Russian areas. Another reason for *korenizatsiya* was the low level of literacy and the difficulty of communicating. Only 45 per cent of the USSR's adult population of 110 million were literate. To explain the advantages of socialism a national education system would be needed. Where there existed indigenous teachers, instruction could be in the local language. If there were no local teachers, instruction would have to be in Russian.

Stalin did not see eye to eye with Lenin on this. Given the opportunity Stalin would have abolished all national differences. At the 13th Congress Stalin accepted Lenin's view that Great Russian chauvinism was a threat but added that local nationalism was also a threat. The Congress did not agree and stated that Great Russian chauvinism and not local nationalism posed the greater threat to the construction of socialism in the USSR. In March 1929 Stalin came up with the concept of the socialist nation. A socialist nation would pass through three stages, each corresponding to a particular stage in the development of socialism. The first stage, the period of socialist construction, would see the nationalities blossom, overcoming their backwardness. They would then qualify as socialist nations. They would then develop fully. National differences and languages would begin to fade away and be replaced by a world language only when the world socialist system was in place.

Russification

Korenizatsiya was abandoned by the Party at the 17th Congress in 1934

- Russification

when the policy of Russification was adopted. In 1929 Stalin wrote about the possibility of 'several zonal economic centres for separate groups of nations, with a separate common language for each group of nations' emerging. The Bolsheviks now believed that the victory of socialism in one country, the USSR, was now possible. This implied that Russian would become the common language of the Soviet zone and that the traditional social structures of the non-Russian nationalities had to be broken up. Moscow was taken aback by the growth of nationalism in the non-Russian areas and how resistant they were to change. Hence, the nations were viewed as socialist nations and had arrived at the stage where they would begin to draw closer to one another and minimise differences.

After 1934 the main threat to the harmonious development of Soviet society changed from Great Russian chauvinism to bourgeois nationalism, which was seen as a disease infesting 'Party and government apparatuses in the Union and Autonomous Republics'. Stalin withdrew his support from the new élites in the national regions and called on them to promote new Party cadres to power. He stated that local nationalism had to be combated. This reversal of policy can be seen to be a return to Stalin's views on the nationality question before 1917.

Four tactics were used by the centre to deal with the problem of local nationalism. Collectivisation, which attempted to destroy local power relationships, the migration of Russians and Ukrainians to non-Slav areas, the spread of Russian as the language of technology and the purging (often the killing) of national élites. Collectivisation and industrialisation sharply increased the demand for qualified personnel in the traditional areas, especially where there were abundant natural resources. Between 1926 and 1939 the Russian proportion of the population of Kazakhstan rose from 19.7 per cent to 40.3 per cent. Graduates were normally assigned to republics other than their own. Most non-Russian graduates were sent to the industrial areas of Russia and Ukraine. Russian became the 'language of friendship', Russian became a compulsory subject in all non-Russian schools in 1938 and the Party decided, also in 1938, to introduce the Russian Cyrillic alphabet for all non-Russian languages (excluding Georgian and Armenian). When compulsory national service was introduced, Russian became the only language of command and this meant the end of all the national units within the Red Army. The expression of Great Russian chauvinism is replaced by the Great Russian people and the concept of Soviet patriotism appears, suggesting that a Soviet identity was emerging.

Stalin did succeed in forging Party and government élites which did not challenge the integrity of the Soviet Union and became loyal to it. Their positions depended on the further existence of the USSR and they were ne beneficiaries of the system. However, nationalism remained and transferred to the local cultural élites who attempted to preserve their own language and culture. This was particularly so in Georgia.

The World Outside the Soviet Union

To Marx a socialist state with a foreign policy was a contradiction in terms, socialist states would have fraternal relations and would not see one another as foreign. The Bolsheviks found themselves as a socialist state in an imperialist sea. Their task was to ensure that bourgeois states did not terminate the Bolshevik experiment. Lenin never gave up hope that he would live to see world revolution. After all, the language of the Comintern under Lenin was German, in preparation for the great day when Berlin would become the world capital. Lenin spoke of communists cohabiting with capitalists, sooner or later the capitalists might attack. During the negotiations which resulted in the treaty of Brest-Litovsk Trotsky was quite aggressive and arrogant, giving the German generals lessons in Hegelian dialectical thought.

What were Russia's priorities during the negotiations which led to the treaty of Brest-Litovsk?

- Lenin advocated peace at any price. He regarded securing Soviet power as the most important priority. Concessions now could be regained later when the socialist revolution broke out. Hence, any concession to Imperial Germany was justified if it secured peace.
- Bukharin and the left communists regarded revolution as the number one priority. They wanted revolutionary war which would ignite Europe and the world. Lenin asked simply: 'where is our army? Bukharin agreed that the communists had no army but believed that revolutionary enthusiasm would produce one that would be irresistible.
- Trotsky accepted that world revolution had to be the top priority but was hesitant about a high risk policy of promoting armed struggle. He did not want to make concessions to Imperial Germany so came up with the policy of neither war nor peace.

The treaty of Brest-Litovsk was of great significance for Soviet Russia. It ended the war with Germany and its allies and ensured that Russia would not be occupied. It provided a breathing space for Lenin to consolidate Soviet power. It ended the prospect of the Reds' enemies linking up with Germany. The debate on whether to sign the treaty had torn the leadership apart. Now the wounds could be healed and the Party strengthened.

The Bolsheviks were lucky that Germany was defeated in November 1918 otherwise a victorious Germany would have come back and extracted greater concessions from Soviet Russia, even taking it over.

After Brest-Litovsk the Reds found themselves consumed by a civil war and had little energy to devote to promoting revolution abroad. However, they did provide money and advice but no men. The expansion of the revolution became a possibility again in 1920 when the Russians

advanced into Poland. Their defeat there meant that they could not intervene outside their frontiers and had to content themselves with providing money and advice.

Frontiers

Soviet Russia paid little attention to its frontiers, expecting other states to join it. Lenin acknowledged the independence of Finland, in December 1917, but saw this as an interim arrangement until the Finnish comrades took power and Finland came back into the fold. Poland had declared independence immediately after the October Revolution, without waiting to consult Lenin. Georgy Chicherin, a former Tsarist diplomat, took over from Trotsky as people's commissar for foreign affairs in March 1918 and adopted a more orthodox attitude towards diplomacy. The setting up of the Comintern meant a second institution concerned with foreign affairs. The Comintern allowed the Bolsheviks to argue that if foreign governments objected to the activities of the Comintern, Soviet Russia could not help as it did not control the world communist organisation (this was a lie as the Comintern was in Moscow and was dominated and later controlled by the Russians).

Bolshevik attitudes towards foreign affairs changed in 1920 after the defeat of the Red Army in Poland where they had expected to be welcomed as liberators but were seen by the Poles as traditional Russian imperialists. The people's commissariat of foreign affairs then began to act independently of the Comintern and began to sign treaties with all neighbouring states defining frontiers. The defeat of the communist republics in Germany and Hungary meant that the Soviet Union was on its own by 1923. World revolution was off the agenda of world politics.

'A spectre [of revolution] is haunting Europe.' A drawing by Deni, 1924

Stalin deftly used Trotsky's view that Soviet Russia could never build socialism on its own or be secure until the world socialist revolution had been victorious against him in their struggle for power. Stalin came up with socialism in one country and derided Trotsky for lack of faith in Russia and also being a gambler who was willing to put the gains of Soviet power at risk in the search for world revolution. Stalin struck a responsive chord among Russians by saying they could make socialism on their own. His Russia first policy was much more attractive than Trotsky's world first policy.

The Failure of World Revolution

The defeat of attempts by communists to take power in Germany in 1923 ended the period of revolutionary hope for the Bolsheviks. They now knew they were on their own and that they would have to build up strong defences for the day when the imperialists would attack. They were not in two minds about this, they were certain war would come. The skill of Bolshevik diplomacy, therefore, had to be deployed to prevent the capitalists uniting against Russia. As Lenin said, communists had to exploit the contradictions among the capitalists.

The first breakthrough came with the treaty of Rapallo which brought together the two outcasts of Europe, Russia and Germany. The treaty led to trade agreements but, more importantly, to military co-operation. The German *Reichswehr* and the Russian Red Army collaborated in Russia. This allowed Germany to circumvent the provisions of the treaty of Versailles, the goal of which was to ensure that Germany never again posed a threat to European peace. There was especially close collaboration between tank, artillery and air force units. As the Great Patriotic War was to demonstrate, the Russians learnt more from these contacts than the Germans.

The Arrival of Fascism

The Wall Street crash of October 1929 led to a crisis of the capitalist system. However, Moscow misread the situation and believed that this meant the final collapse of capitalism. Hence, Moscow and the Comintern (by this time the Comintern took orders from Stalin) attacked the German social democrats in their attempts to save the Weimar republic and linked up with Hitler's national socialists (Nazis) to undermine them. However, out of capitalism's crisis came the monster of Fascism, virulently anti-communist, a much more dangerous beast than the placid capitalism of the 1920s. In 1934 Hitler ended military collaboration with the Red Army.

The Communist Response: the Popular Front

The Comintern saw the danger in 1935 and switched from attacking social democracy to promoting an alliance with social democrats and, indeed, all other democrats against the rising tide of Fascism. This was called a

Popular Front policy. This did not go down very well as, shortly before, social democrats were being called class traitors. Hence, there was very little trust between communists and non-communists and little chance of the Popular Front succeeding.

Stalin's main priority in foreign policy was to avoid involvement in any future European or any other war. He was faced with two main options: either join with other European powers against Germany or join with Germany against the rest of Europe. The weakness of the first option was that it could drag Soviet Russia into a future European war. The second option was appealing. Why should Moscow not reach an agreement with Berlin and set the dogs of war loose in Europe? After all, a second European war would most likely have the same outcome as the first, exhaustion on all sides. A Europe which had destroyed itself by war would find socialism - which would abolish war as wars between socialist states were inconceivable - a most attractive option. That would make Russia the dominant power in Europe. This very appetising menu consisted of various courses:

1 Reach agreement with Hitler, which would give him a free hand in Europe and banish the fear of his attacking Russia;
2 Wait on the sidelines when war inevitably broke out;
3 Wait until Europe had exhausted itself;
4 Send in the Red Army as 'liberators' from capitalism and imperialism;
5 Set up regimes friendly to Moscow; and
6 Carry out a socialist revolution in these countries. This would not be difficult as Soviet Russia had plenty of experience in introducing socialism to the non-Russians under its control.

Stalin may have reached the conclusion that an agreement with Hitler was the preferred option as early as 1936. Stalin, as always, kept his options open. The Comintern pursued a Popular Front policy and Moscow proposed collective security, joining the League of Nations in 1934. However, in its negotiations it never committed itself to helping any state against Germany unless others came in as well. A case in point was the agreement with Czechoslovakia, signed in May 1935. The Czechoslovaks were informed in April 1938 (after the German occupation of Austria on 17 March) that the Soviet Union would only come to the aid of Czechoslovakia if France did the same. The Munich agreement between Germany, Italy, Britain and France, signed in September 1938, which gave Germany the Sudetenland, the German speaking party of Czechoslovakia may have convinced Stalin that the European powers would not fight Hitler. This meant that there was little point in basing Soviet security on agreements with Britain and France. In May 1939 Litvinov, a Jew, gave way to Molotov as people's commissar for foreign affairs. On 24 July 1939 Britain, France and the Soviet Union initial a political agreement i

Moscow which foresaw mutual aid in case of direct or indirect aggression. An Anglo-French military mission negotiated in Moscow from 11-23 August 1939 about the details of military aid. However, the real negotiations were being simultaneously conducted with the Germans and this resulted in the non-aggression pact of 23 August 1939 (this pact is referred to as the Molotov-Ribbentrop Pact, the Nazi-Soviet Pact and the Stalin-Hitler Pact).

This agreement revealed that Stalin had acted in the interests of the Soviet state, not in the interests of socialism. Another example of Stalin's foreign policy was the Spanish Civil War (1936-9) where his goal was to ensure that the Spanish communists did not come to power. Since they were closer to Trotsky than him, a Trotskyist Spain would have spelled disaster for Stalin.

Communist Foreign Policy

A communist state always conducts a two-pronged foreign policy. On the one hand it has to protect its own national interests but, on the other, it wishes to support those communists abroad whose goal is a Moscow-style state. These objectives are often contradictory but when they do clash Soviet Russia always chose to place its own national interests first. Stalin would defend his pact with Hitler (from a communist point of view entering into an agreement with the devil) on the grounds that it was necessary, in the short term, to protect the gains of socialism. The benefits would come in the long term since war in Europe would almost certainly hasten the approach of socialism there. For some reason Stalin trusted Hitler (they never met) to keep his side of the bargain which, of course, Hitler never had any intention of keeping. Stalin judged that his pact with Hitler was a low risk policy (low risk of Russia becoming embroiled in a European war) but it turned out to be high risk and almost destroyed the Soviet Union.

Questions to Consider

- Examine the differences between Lenin's and Stalin's nationality policy.
- Why did local nationalism grow during the 1930s?
- What is a nation, a nation state and nationalism?
- What were the advantages to Soviet Russia of having two institutions concerned with foreign policy - the commissariat of foreign affairs and the Comintern? What were the disadvantages?
- Was Stalin's foreign policy successful?

EXAMINATION QUESTIONS

1 Outline government policies to non-Russians in the former Tsarist lands in the period 1917-39 and assess their success.

2 How important was Russia/the USSR in the foreign policy of western European states between 1918 and 1941?

8 The Historiography of Russian History, 1917-41

Understanding and Interpreting Russian History, 1917-1941

The Soviet Union is no more, it collapsed in 1991. The great Soviet experiment failed. All writing on the Soviet Union before 1991 assumed it would continue but would change. It was a viable state. The collapse forces everyone to reconsider what went wrong. What were the strengths of the country which ensured it lasted for 74 years - the normal life span of a male in Great Britain? What were its weaknesses which led to its demise? Was it born deformed and with congenital birth defects which condemned it to death or, if different policies had been adopted, would it still be alive? Much writing on the Soviet Union was partisan, either the writer supported the goals of the Soviet Union or they were rejected, often vehemently. Marxism, Leninism, and what they spawned, the planned economy, have turned out to be utopian. Lenin understood from the very beginning that the struggle between socialism and capitalism would be to the death, the world was not big enough for both. He also perceived that the main battleground was economic, the system which delivered higher living standards would win. The key to this was higher labour productivity, greater output per worker. By 1991 Soviet labour productivity was less than a third of developed capitalist states.

Theories About the Reasons for Bolshevik Success in 1917

The Orthodox Soviet View

The revolution was inevitable, given the contradictions of capitalism, it was only a matter of when it occurred in Russia. Lenin's writings and leadership were of crucial importance. Russian workers, supported by the poor peasantry, and led by the Bolshevik Party, seized power and set up a worker state.

The Non-Bolshevik Socialist Point of View

The revolution in February 1917 gave rise to a genuinely democratic movement which embraced many differing socialist points of view - it was a pluralist democratic socialist movement. The Bolsheviks put an end to this democratic development when they hijacked the movement, using the language of democracy and socialism but in reality opposing both, and installed their own dictatorship.

The Orthodox Menshevik Point of View

Talk of a worker state in Russia in 1917 was nonsense, given the low level of industrial development and, consequently, the small number of workers. There was no way Russia could develop into a democratic socialist state by the Bolsheviks taking power and instituting their dictatorship. They deployed the language of democracy and socialism while emptying it of any content.

The Successfully Modernising Point of View

Tsarist Russia was successfully transforming itself and adapting to the demands of the industrial age. It was quite capable of developing into a modern, democratic industrially successful state. The First World War, between 1914-17, fatally weakened it as it had not reached the level of maturity to fight a modern war. The Bolsheviks, acting in the interests of Imperial Germany, hammered the final nail into the coffin.

The Failed Modernisation Point of View

Tsarist Russia before 1914 and also during the war was expanding economically and adapting to the demands of the modern industrial world. However, its political structure failed to keep pace with economic change and proved quite inept at managing the modernising state. Given the strains of war, it was likely that a dictatorship would emerge to defend and develop the country. It turned out that the Bolsheviks possessed the skill and appeal to grasp this opportunity.

The Crane Brinton View of Revolution

The American scholar Brinton argues that all modern revolutions go through three main phases: first, the overthrow of the existing system, then a period of moderation, then following by dictatorship and terror.

The Chamberlin Point of View

William Chamberlin, the American historian, in the 1930s, reacting to the prevalent western view that the Bolsheviks were an unrepresentative minority, who seized power by force and kept it by force, argued that Bolshevik success was due to the support of the poor and desperate industrial workers.

The Trotskyist View of the Unfinished Revolution

Trotsky and his supporters regard October 1917 as a genuine workers' revolution which was subsequently hijacked by Stalin and his cohorts for their own selfish ends. They imposed a dictatorship over the working class.

The Social History Point of View

This avoids examining high politics - the politics of power - and concentrates on examining social support for the revolution and its goals by concentrating on those social groups which have benefited from the revolution.

The Soviet Gorbachev-era Point of View

Under *glasnost* (openness) Soviet scholars began criticising Stalin and Stalinism and then Lenin in their search for the roots of dictatorship in the Soviet Union. Dmitry Volkogonov, a military man turned historian, and others, saw a direct link between the dictatorial nature of Lenin and Lenin's Russia and the rise of Stalinism. The October Revolution was not a democratic revolution, it was a vehicle for the dictatorial tendencies of Lenin and the Bolsheviks.

Before considering the system which Stalin developed, Stalinism, let us think about Stalin's priorities.

What Were Stalin's Priorities?

- To keep power.
- Strengthen his position so that no one could challenge him for the position of boss.
- Increase the security of the country so that no country or group of countries would attack the Soviet Union.
- Develop heavy industry (iron, steel, energy, etc) because this expanded the industrial base of the country but also increased the country's ability to produce military hardware.
- Develop a modern transport and communications network.
- Create reliable (willing to obey Stalin's orders) armed forces and police.
- Train a new technical intelligentsia (engineers and managers) who would strive to achieve the goals of the Five Year Plans.
- Raise the efficiency of the government in implementing the goals of the Five Year Plans.
- Produce a Communist Party which was inspired by the political, economic and social goals laid down by Stalin and willing to engage in selfless labour to achieve them.
- Refine Marxist-Leninist-Stalinist ideology so that it corresponded to the needs of the moment and signalled clearly to the population what was expected of them, inspiring them to achieve these goals. One of these goals was to increase labour productivity constantly.
- Eliminate internal opposition to the goals of the Five Year Plans and to Stalin as leader.
- Sovietise (Russify) the non-Russian nationalities and transform them into resourceful allies of Moscow. This implied wiping out local (bourgeois) nationalism and upgrading the role of Russian as the language of communication.
- Expand the influence of communists outside the Soviet Union and ensure that they were reliable allies of the Soviet Union.
- Split the capitalist camp to ensure that they did not united against the

Soviet Union. One tactic was to stress the need for peace, the Soviet Union was tireless in the fight for peace, etc.

What Came Low Down on Stalin's List of Priorities?

- Raising living standards (wealth should be channelled into investment not consumption).
- Improving living conditions by building more dwellings.
- The growth of light industry which produced consumer goods should always be slower than the growth of heavy industry.
- Social justice: the need to build up a strong state took precedence.
- Democracy: only one opinion was legitimate, that of the leader.
- Religious observance: religion was systematically to be stamped out
- A wide, general education: education was to be narrow and geared to producing specialists who only studied their specialty.
- Developing moral values: morality was relative, if it served the revolution it was moral, if not, it was immoral.
- Public opinion: the state should be guided by what was needed to develop it, not by what people wanted. Of course, public opinion did have an impact and forced changes in certain policies but this only concerned the speed and direction of these policies rather than whether these policies should be dropped or not.
- Developing a law-governed state: Stalin always thought the law should serve the state not dictate to it.
- Accuracy in presenting the facts: the presentation of facts and views should place strengthening the state and the leadership in first place. In other words, never let the facts get in the way of a good story. Lying can be very effective, especially if those listening rarely lie. Present Soviet successes in glowing terms because this improves morale at home and makes it less likely that foreign states will invade.
- Never report disasters, defeats, accidents, corruption, conflict within the ruling élite, always present the leadership as united. It is quite unnecessary to report policy discussions at the top. The greater the secrecy, the greater the feeling of mystery and that those at the top are special people, unlike other mortals. Never report the personal lives of those in important positions. Keep secret their perks such as privileged housing, access to consumer goods, holidays, etc.
- The media (press, radio) are there to glorify the progress achieved and inspire even more effort. The task of the media and literary output is not to stimulate a discussion but to make it easier to achieve plan goals.

Now Let Us Attempt a Definition of Stalin's System, Stalinism

This definition is by Roi Medvedev, a Russian who wrote much about the origins of Stalinism - after Stalin's death, of course. This analysis would not have been tolerated under Stalin. It turned Medvedev into a dissident in the Soviet Union. He, however, rejected this term because he saw himself as a loyal communist.

> Stalinism was the cult of the state and the worship of rank, the irresponsibility of those who held power and the population's lack of rights, the hierarchy of privileges and the canonisation of hypocrisy, the barrack (only orders) system of social and intellectual life, the suppression of the individual and the destruction of independent thought, the environment of suspicion and terror, the atomisation of people and notorious 'vigilance', the uncontrolled violence and the legalised cruelty.

Graeme Gill, an Australian Political Scientist, Defines Stalinism:

i) A formally highly centralised, directive economic system characterised by mass mobilisation and an overriding priority on the development of heavy industry;

ii) A social system initially characterised by significant fluidity, most particularly in the form of high levels of social mobility which brings the former lower classes into positions of power and privilege; subsequent consolidation of the social structure results in the dominance of rank, status and hierarchy;

iii) A cultural and intellectual sphere in which all elements are meant to serve the political aims laid down by the leadership and where all areas of culture and intellectual production are politically monitored;

iv) A personal dictatorship resting upon the use of terror as an instrument of rule and in which the political institutions are little more than the instrument of the dictator;

v) All spheres of life are politicised, hence, within the scope of state intervention;

vi) The centralisation of authority is paralleled by a significant measure of weakness of continuing central control, resulting in a system which, in practice, is in its daily operations loosely controlled and structured; and

vii) The initial revolutionary ethos is superseded by a profoundly conservative, status quo, orientation.

Other Approaches: the Totalitarian and New Social Historians

Let us examine two leading schools of thought. One group adopts the totalitarian approach, stressing the goal of Stalin was to achieve total control over the Soviet Union and its people. The other can be referred to as the new social historians. The latter group avoids high politics and concentrates on politics from below, those groups which gained from the October Revolution, through upward social mobility. The new social historians can also be called the revisionists, since they sought to revise the dominant view of the Soviet Union, held until the 1960s.

Concept	Totalitarians	New Social Historians
State	The State is strong, deploying coercion on a massive scale; the objective being to mobilise a victimised, weak society.	State coercion was not to oppress society but a response to managing the great social fluidity of the period.
Society	Reacts, seeking to resist, evade, subvert or through passive resistance, neuter the demands of the state.	Society is dynamic because new hierarchies, new privileges and levels of status, vertical and horizontal cleavages were emerging. Stalinism has some social as well as political dynamics.
Education	Lay great stress on the state control of education, the mass media and propaganda in producing social consent through mass indoctrination.	The indoctrination of society was part and parcel of the process, whereby society acquired the training and culture needed in the new era of socialism.
Mass mobilisation	The Soviet state lacked sophisticated institutions through which to channel social grievances. It used campaigns skilfully to put pressure on bureaucrats, factory managers and so on. These campaigns also helped to identify potential recruits to the Party and state apparatus.	The positive aspects of mass mobilisation are stressed and the negative sides neglected.
Approach to the analysis of the state	Politics from above, the actions of the state, the techniques deployed to achieve the stated goals of the state, the personnel involved and the tensions and conflicts engendered by these goals.	Politics from below, the actions of the state are not studied. Emphasis is placed on the dynamics of the relationships between the different social strata and classes, the prevalent social distinctions and their significance for the lives of individuals, the ways in which individuals can improve their status and protect themselves, the various aspects and repercussions of social mobility, and the ways that some features of the social hierarchy can persist or emerge in spite of, rather than because of, the actions of the regime. What do the new social historians study in order to find answers to the above? Sheila Fitzpatrick researches mass education, social mobility, cultural revolution and the revolutionary continuity from October 1917 to the first Five Year Plan. Getty writes on radical tendencies within

Concept	Totalitarians	New Social Historians
		the Party which was seeking to bring bureaucracy under the control of a mobilised grass roots democracy. Manning writes on participatory management in collective farms. Viola writes on the working-class enthusiasm for the collectivisation campaign. What unites these and other new social historians is that they are broadly sympathetic to the goals of Soviet society.
Terror	Terror is an integral part of Stalinism, directed from above.	Terror is a response to the need to restrain society. Such is the dynamism, volatility and mobility of society that there was a risk it could have devolved in anarchy. Rittersporn, a Russian émigré scholar, sees the origins of the terror in the ungovernability of the country due to bureaucratic infighting and conflict between Moscow and the regions. Getty, an American historian, sees the purges not as bureaucracy trying to stamp out dissent and annihilating old radical revolutionaries but something approaching just the opposite, a radical reaction to bureaucracy, The entrenched office holders were destroyed from above and below in a chaotic wave of revolutionary fervour.
The role of Stalin	The key figure, masterminding the actions of state officials.	Just one of the actors who played a role in the drama of factional conflict.

Critics of the Approach of the New Social Historians

The main critics are members of the totalitarian school, first and foremost Robert Conquest. However, there are many other critics. They all attack the decision of the new social historians to divorce their studies from high politics as if Stalin and the leadership hardly existed. One fierce critic is Moshe Lewin, a Russian émigré scholar. Lewin regards the 1930s as a disaster of epic proportions as the Stalinist state established a proliferation of bureaucratic institutions in an attempt to stabilise the quicksand society it had created by its own destructive campaigns. Lewin sees Stalin as a demon, with his roots in peasant culture, but the new historians regard this demonic nature as a myth.

Overview

The Stalinist state was paradoxically strong and weak. It was strong because it controlled all the levers of power, could deploy coercion, controlled the mass media and so on. It was weak because of the concentration of decision-making at the centre and this stifled local initiative and indeed willingness to take responsibility. It was literally impossible to take all decisions at the centre, so decisions were taken locally and the state found it difficult to monitor developments. The market economy's allocative and distributive functions had to be taken over by central and local government and this multiplied bureaucracy as the economy expanded. How was Stalin to check on whether the government was doing its job? He handed the task over to the political police. There was an attempt to remove officials in 1936-8 and replace them with a new generation from the working class and peasantry who were viewed as more politically reliable, untouched by previous political conflicts and with some industrial and technical experience. The totalitarians conceded that the very fact that Stalin and the leadership attempted to put in place a new generation of officials reveals the conservatism of entrenched officials and the difficulty of manipulating them from above.

Other Approaches

Given the shortcomings of the approaches of the totalitarians and the new social historians, it is worth attempting an approach which integrates political and social policies. Martin McCauley has suggested the reconstruction-consolidation or 'reccon' approach. This views the history of the Soviet Union as a series of advances and retreats in order to consolidate gains. Revolution and war communism were an advance; NEP was a retreat to permit the Bolsheviks to build up their strength before they attempted another advance; 1928-32 was a whirlwind advance; 1933-6 was a temporary slow-down to consolidate; 1937-9 was another violent advance; 1939-41 was less radical with the ending of the purges, and then war intervened.

The reccon approach gives due weight to the power of the state but also takes into consideration social resistance to official policy. This explains the need for periods of consolidation. The crisis of 1932-3, the terrible famine in Ukraine and the slow-down in growth rates, all of which put Stalin's position in jeopardy, made necessary the period of consolidation which followed. Recent research has revealed that Stalin and Molotov were convinced that there was widespread opposition to the regime in the 1930s and that this could become critical in time of war. This may explain the purge of the Red Army of 1937-8.

Trotsky's interpretation of Stalin has been influential. He found parallels with the French Revolution and wrote of Thermidorian reaction and bureaucratic degeneration. On Thermidor 9 (27 July 1794) Robespierre and other Jacobin leaders were overthrown and the French Revolution degenerated into reaction. The failure of revolution abroad led to the gradual demise of the revolution at home. Russia's small working class could not elevate the gains of October into a fully functioning democratic dictatorship of the proletariat. Instead, the Party-state machine placed itself above society and took control of politics, administration and the manufacture and distribution of scarce goods An army of commissars, enterprise managers and Party functionaries took control and ran the state in their own interests. Trotsky did not blame Lenin but the 'dialectics of history' (fate) had thrown up Stalin who was aided and abetted by his minions, the dross, the flotsam, the sneaks, the worms who were crawling out of the upturned soil of the manured revolution. Stalinism, in Trotsky's view, could not last. He was right but he did not live to see it. Stalin made sure of that.

Isaac Deutscher, a Polish supporter of Trotsky, broadly accepts this picture. He did not consider Stalin a great politician or even one approaching greatness. He was very ordinary. It was the machine which made and kept Stalin in power. Stalin was not inevitable, others could have guided Soviet Russia towards socialism.

E.H. Carr, the British historian, sees Stalin as an ordinary political figure borne along by the dynamic forces of the revolution. Industrialisation was inevitable so someone would have taken on the task. It just happened to be Stalin. Carr has a higher opinion of Stalin but he still sees him as being moulded by the times rather than moulding the times. The excesses of the cult of the personality were unfortunate but they were not strong enough to negate the dynamic forces which were propelling the revolution forward. Carr comes close to arguing that Stalinism happened because it had to happen. Therefore competing visions of socialism in Soviet Russia are irrelevant. Carr does not waste any time considering whether Bukharin's views would have produced something different. Moral judgements and discussions about alternative routes to socialism are idle speculation.

Roi Medvedev views Stalinism as pseudo-socialism. Stalin took Lenin's noble vision of the Soviet Union and corrupted and distorted it.

Alexander Solzhenitsyn does not recognise Stalinism as a phenomenon since Stalin was the blind, mechanical executor of Lenin's will. It follows he has a low opinion of Lenin as well.

Questions to Consider

- How do totalitarians analyse the Soviet Union?
- Why do they place so much emphasis on Stalin's personality and his actions?
- Why do the new social historians avoid high politics and concentrate on politics from below?
- Which approach do you find more enlightening?
- Are alternative approaches more enlightening?

9 Russia, 1917-41 Continuity and Change

Soviet Russia, in 1941, was unique in Europe, it was the only state which claimed to be Marxist socialist (there was only one other such state in the world at that time, Mongolia). It claimed to be applying the insights gained from Marx's writings so as to build the most successful state on Earth. The more successful the Soviet Union became the more attractive it would become as a model for other states, especially those which wished to modernise and industrialise. This applied to most of the world, since developed capitalist states could be counted on the fingers of two hands. Moscow, therefore, was different. It was developing internally according to its own priorities but externally it was in intense competition with capitalist states.

Soviet Russia was building a new type of state, one based on the common ownership of the means of production (factories and farms), distribution (trade) and exchange (banks).

Soviet Russia

What claims did it make for itself?	What was the real situation in 1941?
• It was the most successful economy in the world.	• The Soviet Union was a successful economy but not exceptional (average annual growth of 5.1 per cent). It had a long way to go before it could challenge the US.
• Collectivised agriculture was the most advanced in the world.	• Collectivised agriculture was a great disappointment and remained the weakest sector of the Soviet economy until 1991.
• It was forging ahead of the capitalist world.	• The Soviet Union was already ahead of some capitalist countries but not the leaders.
• It had eliminated trade cycles, which resulted in the ups and downs of economic growth elsewhere.	• It was not subject to international trade cycles as it was not dependent on foreign trade since it had everything it needed at home, except rubber.

What claims did it make for itself?	What was the real situation in 1941?
• Power in the Soviet Union was in the hands of the working class and the collective farm peasantry - they ran the country.	• The claim that power in the Soviet Union was in the hands of the workers and peasants was a myth. Power rested with Stalin and the leadership.
• It was the only true democracy in the world.	• Democracy in the Soviet Union was defined as the working class and peasantry in power. Since this was not so, the claim that the Soviet Union was a democracy was also a myth. Democracy in the western sense, pluralist democracy, did not exist and could not exist (it came near to it in 1989-91).
• The exploitation of the working man and woman had ended.	• Arguably, life was harder for working men and women in the 1930s than before 1917. They had fewer rights, the right to strike was theoretically there but it was not advisable to claim it. Living standards for workers were lower in 1941 than 1917.
• Unemployment was a thing of the past.	• There was little unemployment except in Central Asia and Transcaucasia.
• Living standards were constantly rising.	• Living standards were rising but from a low base and had not yet attained the level of 1914.
• Educational levels were rising.	• Educational levels were rising, one of the great achievements of the Soviet period.
• Cultural levels were rising.	• Cultural levels, judging by literacy, were rising.
• Crime was disappearing.	• Crime was not declining, indeed it was rising.
• Religion was disappearing.	• Religious observance was declining because so many churches had been closed. However, faith continued in private.

What claims did it make for itself?	What was the real situation in 1941?
• The nationality (non-Russians) problem had finally been solved.	• The nationality problem posed problems for Stalin during the 1930s and his change of course in 1934 testifies to the problem of local nationalism. Non-Russians never accepted the Soviet goal of merging with all nations, with the Russian nation first.
• The Soviet Union would never attack another state, it was a peace-loving state.	• The Soviet Union attacked Poland and Finland in 1939 and invaded Estonia, Latvia and Lithuania in 1940 without any fighting. Nevertheless, Soviet foreign policy until 1941 was defensive and geared towards maintaining peace.
• The Soviet Union rejected imperialism and had liberated all the non-Russians within the country.	• Many non-Russians regarded the Russians as imperialists, for example, the Estonians, Latvians and Lithuanians.
• The victory of socialism worldwide was inevitable and the example of the Soviet Union would play an important part in this victory.	• The number of Marxist-Leninist states reached its peak in the 1970s but afterwards declined. The collapse of the Soviet Union in 1991 led to the end of the world communist movement.

This is a mixed record. However, there was great optimism in the Soviet Union by 1941 that it was becoming one of the great states of the world. Stalin's greatest achievement was to strengthen the country to the point that it was capable of defeating Nazi Germany (1941-5). That was a truly astounding performance and the rest of Europe will always be in his debt for it. In 1945 Soviet Russia was a world power and, by the mid-1970s, it was a superpower.

Stalin's Russia succeeded in mobilising the population to achieve great goals but at a fearful cost in human life. Then there was the huge waste and inefficiency. When Stalin died Khrushchev tried to reform the system he inherited but unsuccessfully. Gorbachev tried again and blew the whole system up. This points to the fact that Stalin's system suited Russia and Russians. It engendered élites who had a stake in the system. That was its strength and weakness. Cut off from the rest of the world economy because Russia did not need to export to survive, these Party and government officials and managers did not see why they should change and risk losing

their privileges. The Stalinist economy was well suited to achieving certain objectives but at the cost of the growth of the whole economy. Heavy industry and defence dominated and deformed the whole structure of industry. Coercing peasants into collective farms did not lead to their willingness to work. The major problem which always faced socialist agriculture was how to motivate the work force. The answer in all other countries is to give them land to farm for themselves but this solution could not be adopted by Moscow as it would have signalled the return of capitalism.

Stalin: The Red Tsar? How Much Change Was There?

From the point of view of government and administration was Soviet Russia very different from Tsarist Russia in 1914? They were remarkably similar. Power and decision-making were concentrated at the centre with a strong leader. Stalin was called the *vozhd,* the boss. The state in 1941 was much stronger. The ministries (people's commissariats) implemented the plans and the local enterprises had little say in what and how things were produced. The Soviet state was a much more bureaucratic state with many more officials than in 1917. This was because it was more ambitious and was mobilising the population to achieve economic goals. There was rapid economic growth before 1914 by applying the market economy and there was rapid economic growth by 1941 using a planned economy. The Red Army in 1941 was much stronger than the Tsarist Army in 1917. The police and secret police were vastly more numerous in 1941 than in 1917. Culturally, the country in 1917 was pluralist but, in 1941, socialist realism had been imposed and there was uniformity - the arts were to glorify economic achievements and inspire the population to produce more. Russia was evolving into a pluralist democracy in 1917 but, in 1941, it was a one-party dictatorship. Living standards for the vast majority of the population were higher before 1914 than in 1941.

Why did the population put up with it? There were isolated revolts but nothing to threaten the state. Citizens were aware they were living in two worlds and that much of the official propaganda was false. How does one explain their willingness to do so? A British example holds the key. Many borrowers in Britain got into financial difficulties in the 1990s because their properties had lost value and were worth less than their mortgage. Many of them could not meet their mortgage repayments. They got to the point that when they received another letter from the building society, they did not open it but threw it away. They refused to face reality and preferred to live in a nicer world. The same thing applied in the Soviet Union. Life was so grim for so many that if they had been told the truth about Stalin's crimes, the corruption of officials and all the official lies they would probably have refused to believe it, preferring to believe in a better world. This is what kept them going. When bad news was reported for the first time under Gorbachev some older readers were very upset. They said that they did not buy newspapers to read bad news.

Russia had a red Tsar and he was worshipped as a demi-god. One of Stalin's failures symbolises his attempt to change Russia. The Orthodox Church had played a very important role in the evolution of the Russian state, nation and culture. Stalin wanted to move from a spiritual to a secular era. During the 1930s he ordered the destruction of the magnificent cathedral of Christ the Saviour in Moscow and planned to build on its site a vast Palace of Soviets. To the Russian population this was to symbolise the death of the old and the birth of the new Russia. However, when Russian engineers tried to build the new edifice they discovered that it could not be done, the cathedral had been resting on a swamp. The Palace of Soviets was never built (the cathedral was rebuilt and reconsecrated in 1996). Stalin changed Russia on the outside but not on the inside.

Postscript: Post-Gorbachev Russia in the light of Russian History, 1917-41

Mikhail Gorbachev, during an interview in London in October 1996, when asked which event in Russian history he would like to change, stated he would have liked the February Revolution to continue. This breathtaking comment implied that he now regards the whole communist era to have been an aberration. Russia would have been better off without the October Revolution, Lenin, Stalin and everything which followed. Russia since 1991 has found it very difficult to find its way back to Europe, the world market economy and democracy. Industrial production in 1996 was just over half of the level of 1991. However, new political and economic élites have emerged, just like the period 1917-41. Ideology has ebbed away so that power is now mainly derived from economic wealth. After 1917, the communist ruling class, in personnel, was different from the Tsarist era. However, since 1991 over two-thirds of the new ruling class are from the old communist *nomenklatura.* Political power rests with the President, with the Duma or parliament, weak. This duplicates the communist era. However, for the first time in Russian history, the individual has the opportunity to develop his or her talents fully. Gone is the collectivist ideology of communism. Russians are throwing off the remnants of the communist experiment remarkably quickly. Perhaps Stalin's reforms were only cosmetic after all.

Questions to Consider

- Why were the 1930s so violent? The number of those who died during the purges of the 1930s has recently been put at 10-11 million (Alec Nove).
- Why was it necessary for so many to die? Why was support for Stalin so high in 1941 despite his cruelty and violence?
- Is it fair to call Stalin a red Tsar?
- 'Soviet Russia was a well-run state by 1941.' Comment.

Glossary

ASSR Autonomous Soviet Socialist Republic, an administrative unit of a republic which is populated by a nationality other than the titular nationality, eg, the Tatars make up the Tatar ASSR in the RSFSR. Even though they had their own government they were, in reality, run from the republic's capital, in the Tatars' case, Moscow.

Bolsheviks When the Russian Social Democratic Labour (Workers') Party (RSDRP), founded in 1898, split in 1903, those in the majority were called Bolsheviks and those in the minority, Mensheviks.

Brest-Litovsk Treaty with Germany, March 1918, recognised Soviet Russia in international law; fulfilled the Bolshevik promise to bring peace; revealed how split the Bolshevik leadership was after October 1917.

Candidate member i) before a person could become a full member of the Communist Party he/she had to serve a probationary period during which he/she was called a candidate member;
ii) candidate members of the Central Committee and Politburo could attend meetings, speak but not vote.

CC Central Committee of the Communist Party; this organisation acted in the name of the Party Congress when the latter was not in session; it contained all the important Party officials, government ministers, leading army, air force and naval personnel, ambassadors, etc.

CEC Russian Central Executive Committee of the soviets, the body which acted in the name of the Congress of Soviets when that body was not in session. It was the key institution in October 1917 but rapidly lost power to the Party.

Cheka Russian Extraordinary Commission to Fight Counter Revolution, Sabotage and Speculation; established in December 1917; renamed OGPU in 1922; later KGB. Feliks Dzerzhinsky was its leader, 1917-26.

Collectivisation Establishment of collective farms (*kolkhozes*) and state farms (*sovkhozes*) which ended private ownership of land and farming. Collectivisation began voluntarily in 1917 but had made little headway by 1929 when it really got under way; was completed in 1937. In practice, several villages were lumped together and called a *kolkhoz*, peasant opposition being dealt with brutally, by using military force, deportation or expulsion. In March 1930 the private plot around the peasant's house was legalised and it helped to keep rural dwellers alive.

Comintern Communist International; international communist organisation established in 1919 and disbanded in 1943.

Commissar i) government minister; ii) official representing Party, government or soviet.

Conference Differed from a Party Congress in that not all organisations were represented. In the early years the problem of bringing communists together made convening a Congress at short notice difficult. A conference did not have the right to elect members to the CC and Politburo.

Congress Most important meeting of Party, soviet, trade union or other organisation; at a Congress the Party reviewed its past record and laid down goals for the future; a new CC was elected and it, in turn, elected a new Politburo and Secretariat.

FYP Five Year Plan; the first ran from October 1928 to December 1932; the second from January 1933 to December 1937; the third from January 1938 to June 1941.

Gosplan State Planning Commission of Sovnarkom (government), responsible for drafting economic plans and checking on their implementation; founded February 1921; headed by G.M. Krzhizhanovsky, 1921-3, 1925-30; A.D. Tsyurupa, 1923-5; V.V. Kuibyshev, 1930-4; V.I. Mezhlauk, 1934-7; N.A. Voznesensky, 1938-49.

Kolkhoz Collective farm; members farmed the land as a co-operative but in reality had little say in what was to be produced; this was laid down in the annual state plan. If the farm recorded a loss no wages were paid.

Kombedy Committees of poor peasants, set up by Sovnarkom in June 1918 to seize grain from the richer peasants with the state receiving most (this did not happen). In November 1918 there were 122,000 kombedy but they were disbanded the same month.

Komsomol Communist youth organisation for those between 14 and 28.

Kulak (Kulak, in Russian, means fist) Peasants were divided into poor, middle and rich by the Bolsheviks. A rich peasant.

Left communists Bukharin was the leader of this group on the CC (October 1917-18); they favoured the immediate introduction of socialism and a revolutionary war against imperial Germany. Lenin wanted a slow march to socialism and peace with Berlin and eventually had his way.

Mensheviks When the Russian Social Democratic Labour (Workers') Party, founded in 1898, split in 1903, those in the minority were called Mensheviks; in October 1917 the Mensheviks opposed the Bolshevik seizure of power.

Moderate socialists Mensheviks and right Social Revolutionaries; they were moderate compared to the radical Bolsheviks.

NEP New Economic Policy, introduced in March 1921; it brought back the market economy and money being backed by gold; in practice it ended in 1929.

NKVD People's Commissariat of Internal Affairs; political police.

Orgburo Organisational Bureau of the CC; handled all matters of an organisational and administrative nature, domestic and foreign, except those deemed important enough to be passed to the Politburo.

Politburo Political Bureau of the CC; key decision-making body of the Communist Party; established 1919; prior to that the CC was the most important body.

Rabkrin People's Commissariat of Workers' and Peasants' Inspectorate; founded in 1920 to supervise all government organs; dissolved in 1934 when its functions were transferred to the Commission of Soviet Control; in 1940 became the People's Commissariat of State Control; headed by Stalin, 1920-2; A.D, Tsyupura, 1922-3; V.V. Kuibyshev, 1923-6; S. Ordzhonikidze, 1926-30; A.A. Andreev, 1930-4.

RCP(B) Russian Communist Party (Bolsheviks), 1918-25; renamed the Communist Party of the Soviet Union (Bolsheviks), 1925-52.

RSFSR Russian Soviet Federated Socialist Republic; constitution adopted in June 1918; between October 1917 and July 1918 the state was referred to as Soviet Russia or the Russian republic, in essence the RSFSR; when the USSR was founded in December 1922 the RSFSR became the largest republic.

Secretariat The administrative centre of the Communist Party; its key officials were called secretaries and the leading one General Secretary.

Sovkhoz State farm; run like a factory with guaranteed minimum wages higher than those in the collective farms. Employees were classified as workers (unlike collective farm personnel) and qualified for their social benefits.

Soviet Name of the state; also, name of a council.

Sovnarkom The Council of People's Commissars; the government of Soviet Russia and later the USSR. Headed by Lenin, October 1917-January 1924; A.I. Rykov, February 1924-December 1930; V.M. Molotov, December 1930-May 1941; Stalin, May 1941-March 1953.

SRs Social or Socialist Revolutionaries; an agrarian (non-Marxist) socialist party; split in late 1917 into right and left (pro-Bolshevik) SRs; the left SRs joined Sovnarkom in December 1917 to form a coalition government with the Bolsheviks. They left after the signing of the treaty of Brest-Litovsk, which they bitterly opposed; this led to armed violence; both parties were banned in the early 1920s.

State capitalism The economic order between October 1917 and June 1918.

Supreme Soviet Established by the 1936 constitution, the USSR Supreme Soviet had two houses, the Soviet of the Union and the Soviet of Nationalities; the number of deputies of the former was based on the population, the number of the latter was fixed.

USSR Union of Soviet Socialist Republics (the only country in the world not to have a territory included in its name).

VSNKh (Vesenkha) Supreme Council of the National Economy; founded in December 1917 and responsible for the whole economy and state finances; as of June 1918 it became in effect the commissariat of nationalised industry; at the local level a VSNKh ran industry. In 1924 a VSNKh was set up in every republic and made responsible for its industry. Headed by N. Osinsky, 1917-18; A.I. Rykov, 1918-20, 1923-4; P.A. Bogdanov, 1921-3; F.E. Dzerzhinsky, 1924-6; V.V. Kuibyshev, 1926-30; S. Ordzhonikidze, 1930-2; then it was divided into the Commissariats of Heavy Industry, Light Industry and the Timber Industry.

War communism The economic order in place between June 1918 and March 1921.

Further Reading

R. Service, *The Russian Revolution 1900-1927,* Macmillan, 1986, is an admirable survey. See also M. McCauley, *The Soviet Union, 1917-1991,* Longman, 1993. The best book on the origins of the First World War is D.C.B. Lieven, *Russia and the Origins of the First World War,* Macmillan, 1983. O. Figes, *A People's Tragedy. The Russian Revolution 1905-17,* Jonathan Cape, 1996, is excellent. E. Acton, *Rethinking the Russian Revolution,* Edward Arnold, 1990, is a useful commentary on recent scholarship. D. Koenker, *Moscow Workers and the 1917 Revolution,* Princeton U.P. (USA), 1969, is very informative. W. Lincoln, *Red Victory,* New York, 1989, and E. Mawdsley, *The Russian Civil War,* Cambridge U.P., 1987, are good on this topic.

The most scholarly work on Lenin is R. Service, *Lenin: A Political Life,* 3 vols., Macmillan, 1991-5, but needs to be supplemented by R. Pipes, ed., *The Unknown Lenin From the Secret Archive,* Yale U. P. (USA), 1996, which reveals how violent Lenin really was and that Stalin merely continued his work. N. Harding, *Leninism,* Macmillan, 1996, is excellent while T.H. Rigby, *Lenin's Government: Sovnarkom 1917-1922,* Cambridge U.P., 1979, is penetrating.

On Stalin, R. McNeal, *Stalin: Man and Ruler,* Macmillan, 1988, is very good and R. Conquest, *Stalin, The Breaker of Nations,* Weidenfeld and Nicolson, 1991, is stimulating. The industrialisation debate is covered in two volumes by E.H. Carr and R.W. Davies *Foundations of a Planned Economy 1926-1929,* Macmillan, 1969. R.E. Pipes *The Foundation of the Soviet Union,* Harvard U.P. (USA), second edition 1954, analyses the important nationalities topic, a problem which was never solved. On workers, D. Filtzer, *Soviet Workers and Stalinist Industrialisation,* Pluto Press, 1986, is sympathetic to workers and sober reading for believers in Stalin's revolution. On the purges, R. Conquest, *The Great Terror,* Hutchinson, 1990, is the leader among those who believe it was orchestrated from above. J. Arch Getty, *Origins of the Great Purges,* Cambridge U.P., 1985, sees purges to be mainly from below. On Stalin and the Stalinism phenomenon, G. Gill, *Stalinism,* Macmillan, 1990, is a succinct summary. N. Lampert, *Stalinism: Its Nature and Aftermath,* Macmillan, 1991, is excellent and thought provoking.

Collections of documents: M. McCauley, *Octobrists to Bolsheviks 1905-1917,* Edward Arnold, 1984 and *The Russian Revolution and the Soviet State 1917-1921,* Macmillan, 1995, are widely used.

Index

Page numbers in **bold** are primary references, pages in *italics* are in the Chronology